P9-CDV-247

15 00

Successful Striped Bass Fishing

Successful

FRANK T. MOSS

Striped Bass Fishing

WITH SELECTIONS BY **MARK J. SOSIN** /
AL REINFELDER / **CHARLES R. MEYER** /
LARRY GREEN / **HERB DUERKSEN** /
BOB HUTCHINSON / **PETE MCLAIN**

International Marine Publishing Company

CAMDEN, MAINE

DEDICATION

Fishermen learn their trade by their own mistakes and sweat,

but also through the example of other great fishermen.

Eight men, who have made the sundown tow,

especially inspired my understanding of striped bass.

Charles Church

Otto Scheer

Louis Cihlar

Capt. Frank Tuma Sr.

Bob Crandall

Joseph Brooks

Herbert Borchers

Al Reinfelder

To their memory this book is respectfully and affectionately dedicated.

Contents

Special Charts, Tables, and Diagrams

Acknowledgements

Special thanks should be expressed to Robert N. Bavier Jr., Publisher of *Sportfishing* Magazine and President of Yachting Publishing Corp., for permission to use articles originally published in *Sportfishing*.

Thanks are also due to the following writers who have contributed important portions of the book: Herb Duerksen, Bob Hutchinson, Larry Green, Pete McLain, Charles R. Meyer, the late Al Reinfelder, and Mark J. Sosin.

Successful Striped Bass Fishing

Broadway, Bob Sylvester. Sylvester had found bass at a secret spot, and the others were dying to learn where he was catching his fish.

One night Bob handcuffed himself with the hooks of a plug that pulled out of a big striper as he tried to gaff it. Alone and in agony he managed to drive his jeep back to town. While Sylvester was sweating in the doctor's office, waiting for the Novocain to take effect, Sonny Smith was outside examing his muddy jeep. Sonny was sure that mud on the tires could have come only from pot holes in the track leading to Caswell's, a famous striper location.

Smith swore me to secrecy when he invited me and his brother-in-law, Ken Anderson, to prospect Sylvester's suspected secret spot. By a roundabout route we arrived at dusk at the high cliffs above Caswell's, west of Montauk Point. Sonny and Ken immediately took possession of rocks well out in the surf and suggested that I scout the more protected cove to the east.

There, as deep twilight set in, I spotted a monstrous striper.

Outside the first line of breakers, mullet were rippling. Suddenly a shark-like fish slashed through the mullet, scattering them wildly. But no shark has a huge bucket head, dark stripes down each flank, and a big spade tail. It was the biggest striped bass I had ever seen.

I cast my Stan Gibbs darter into the mullet—and fetched a blacklash. As I picked frantically at the mess in the reel, the huge bass rolled on my plug and flipped it into the air with its tail. Finally the blacklash was clear. I took up the slack line, gave the darter a twitch, and held my breath. There was a boil in the water and my plug was gone. As in the slow motion of a dream, I struck hard and got set for a heavy run.

Nothing happened.

There was a fish on my line, but it was no monster. I reeled in the captive and found a school bass just big enough for a supper for two. At that moment the mullet broke again, further out. I tossed the little bass onto the rocks behind me and uncorked a tremendous heave. *Pop* went the line and my only Gibbs darter rocketed off into the gloom. Cursing, I rerigged with metal and fished the spot for an hour without luck.

Sonny and Ken had a half-dozen good fish between them. Later, stocking up on plugs at Kronuch's tackle emporium, I let slip the identity of Sylvester's secret spot. The next night Caswell's was alive with surf fishermen. Sam Cox had his reel stripped when he hooked his bitch, Ginger, on the backswing, but nobody caught any fish. Sylvester's secret blitz was over.

The occasion taught me two valuable lessons: (1) *never let excitement rob you of your cool,* (2) *don't admit to where you catch your stripers.* Of course, in preparing this book, I am breaking the second rule, but I pass it on to you to observe or ignore as you see fit.

During the great boating boom of the late '50's and early '60's, striped bass fishing activity increased to the point where keeping a good spot secret became a real chore. Not only did stripers get under my skin, but also some of my fishing competitors got there too. Fishing success often depended on being a detective on the water.

Charter boat skippers Ralph Pitts and Carl Darenburg were great fishing buddies who delighted in hoodwinking the rest of the fleet. One foggy afternoon they cooked up a scheme to fool the other skippers into thinking they were catching plenty of fish down by Montauk Light while, in reality, they were fishing at another spot several miles away. Their cryptic radio messages were carefully phrased to convey this false impression.

On the most tenuous of suspicions, I put my radio direction finder on them and soon prospered mightily when I found

Surf casters and trolling boats work the Rhode Island sand beach at Charlestown Breachway as the morning sun highlights the foam of a gentle surf.

them guiltily hauling in double-headers of big school bass out on Shagwong Reef.

On a different occasion I shared a two-boat party with another Montauk skipper. The party was for two days and, according to plan, the men were to swap boats on the second day to even the fishing chances. This was when a new type of bucktail jigging lure was starting to make an impression on the fish and the fishermen.

The other captain had been having success with the new jigs, while I had been catching my share with an older type of trolling lure. Getting ready for the first day's fishing, this chap brought over a batch of the new jigs which my party insisted we try. But Jim, my mate, had trouble getting the men to jig the rods properly, and at the end of the day we had only two medium-sized stripers to the other boat's 15 big ones.

The next morning we almost didn't sail. The men on the other boat refused to switch to mine and the men who had fished with me didn't want to do it a second time. They were even less inclined to go when they saw the tackle that Jim and I had prepared for them to use.

After holding a council of war the previous evening, we had decided to abandon the tricky new jigs and go back to lures that we knew and trusted. These were three-ounce Japanese tuna feathers double-hooked with long strips of fresh squid. To handle these huge lures, which were as much as 18 inches long, we had broken out a set of school tuna rods. To get the lures down deep, we had attached a one-pound gooseneck drail to each tuna line, placing a two-fathom wire leader between drail and feather lure.

I finally got the men on board by promising them a free trip if we caught no fish.

The author lifts a 20-pounder on board as Jerry Kenny, at the wheel, pilots their 23-foot Formula off Evans' Rock, just inside Montauk Point.

Out we went to Shagwong Reef, tuna rods with their 6/0 reels stuck into the stern rod holders. The tide was ebbing and knots of herring and blackback gulls were working over spots where squid and whiting were schooling just under the surface. Things looked mighty bassy.

Jim was setting out the last of the tuna rods when, just ahead, big bass started to break among the bait. Immediately a dozen fast boats swooped into the area, rods jigging frantically. A fish or two were hooked.

Slowly, I S-turned the boat through the spot where the other boats had driven the fish down. Jim stood in the stern, ready for action. Suddenly three rods bent in quick succession and line began screaming from the reels. We had hooked a triple-header.

Startled men scrambled from the cabin to grab up the rods. Fifteen minutes later we had three 40-pounders in the stern box. After that, the party was a changed group of men. Sticking to the slow, deep trolling that we knew so well, we caught 18 big fish before it was time to quit. Our men were ecstatic. Jim got a handsome tip and I was well-paid for the day.

Best of all, the self confidence that I regained from our success with the older lures cured me of a case of striper fever that had been driving me up the wall. For weeks, I had been secretly dreading the time when I would have to test the new lures against the old. Now I knew that the stripers, at least, were unimpressed by fancy new lures as long as the old reliables were properly presented.

But the itch always returns.

The last time stripers got under my skin was during a recent Tournament of the Full Moon, the two-day striper marathon held each October at Montauk's Deep Sea Club. I had given up professional charter fishing several years before, and in the intervening time had not wet a line for stripers. My companions were Jerry

Kenny, outdoor editor of the New York *Daily News*, and bass-wise Gene Serafine.

"Frank knows every striper hole on Montauk. He'll get us fish," predicted Gene as we loaded gear into the 23-foot twin-outboard fisherman that had been loaned to us.

Jerry said nothing, but I could visualize him telling himself, "Moss hasn't fished these waters in years. I wonder if he still remembers the old spots."

I was half-psyched into striper fever before we left the dock. Erstwhile fishing buddies had showed me the strange new "umbrella rigs" that harnessed as many as six trolling lures to one line. Nobody jigged anymore. How could you jig with an umbrella frame on the end of your line?

I went ahead and rigged some of the old, reliable feathers, Jigit eels, and Kramer and No Alibi bass bugs that were still in my tackle box, trusting that there might be a few elderly fish left that could appreciate a familiar lure. But we hadn't been fishing for an hour when I knew we were in trouble.

None of the old lures worked. The old fishing ranges, burned like brands on the rawhide of my memory, failed to produce strikes. Instead, the tournament fleet plowed between the lighthouse and Great Eastern Rock in no apparent pattern, steadily dredging up stripers with the newfangled umbrella rigs. I didn't understand what was going on.

Next day was more of the same. We nailed a few small fish with spinning plugs down by Evans Rock, but the big points-earning stripers eluded us. Jerry and Gene were philsosophical, but I could see that they knew I was close to popping my cool. Finally, a last-ditch plan took shape in my mind.

"Let's go in and eat and sleep so we can fish the midnight tide on Shagwong Reef," I suggested. They agreed.

We sailed at 11 P.M., long after the bulk

of the tournament fleet had gone out to fish the glorious moonlit night. I was banking on a practical application of the Biblical injunction that "the last shall be first." We idled down to the reef, lights out, making no noise. Miles to the southeast the lights of the umbrella-dredging fleet looked like a city on the water. We were entirely alone.

I'd rigged Gene with a plain white feather and a strip of fresh squid. Jerry had elected to troll a Creek Chub Pikie, a plug in which he had great faith. I aimed the boat inshore to test the shallow water off Shagwong Point, moving up-tide in eight feet of water. Ahead was a small rip marking a ledge of rocks and the proper place to swing out into deeper water.

I took a breath. We were moving a hair too fast, but better too fast than too slow in this shallow water. Now we were up to the rip. I let the boat coast through, mentally counting off the seconds until the lures would be in the disturbed water. Then I turned the wheel so the lure would rake the rocks as we moved offshore.

Suddenly, *zing-zing!*

"Got one!" rasped Jerry Kenny.

"Me too!" echoed Gene Seafine.

Tension let go of my spine. We completed the offshore turn and I gaffed two 15-pounders. Then we swung down-tide for a fresh pass. I avoided the lone rock where we could hang up and lose a line. The rip was ahead again and I cautioned myself not to turn too soon.

Zing-zing! Another pair. This I could understand.

At two A.M. we were exhausted, the boxes full of good fish. Kenny and Serafine had caught them all. They were like two kids who had helped put the circus to bed.

My satisfaction ran deeper. It came from knowing that indeed I had not forgotten, and that once again I had made these wild, wonderful fish pay for the incurable itch that their tribe had infected me with here on this same reef, more than 30 long years before.

This would hold the fever in check, until the next time.

2 / What Makes Roccus Run?

IF A COMMITTEE OF SPORT FISHERMEN TRIED to design a fish for general popularity, impressive appearance, excellent table qualities, fighting heart, and the indefinable aura of mystery that makes a good fish great, it would be hard-put to do better than nature's very own striped bass, *Roccus saxatilis*.

Here is a fishy-looking fish of handsome profile, robust build, and firm delicious meat, a fish capable of withstanding wide differences of temperature and equipped to live and thrive in the coastal regions of our Atlantic and Pacific oceans near large centers of population.

At this point let me pause to explain my use of the older name *Roccus saxatilis* rather than the newer name *Morone saxatilis* favored by some marine biologists. These scientists may be correct in lumping the striper with other fish of the *Morone* bass clan, but to millions of sport fishermen across the land he is *Roccus*, and thus here he will remain.

The striper is closely related to the white perch (*Morone americana*), a member of the marine bass family that lives in brackish waters in the warmer portions of the striper's Atlantic range. Another close cousin is the white bass of fresh water (*Morone chrysops*), a denizen of our southern and central states. All three species are thought to have descended from common stock, each differentiating along the way as habitat and beneficial mutation favored changes in characteristics. All look a good deal alike to the casual eye, although the striper is by far the largest of the three.

For years it has been a statement of faith among bass anglers that the all-tackle world record is (or was) the 73-pound monster caught by Charles Church in Quick's Hole, Massachusetts, back in 1913. I qualify this statement because at least one other 73-pounder has been landed since then on rod and reel. This was Charles Cinto's record-tying fish, taken off Cuttyhunk Island, Massachusetts, in 1967. An 81-pounder turned up in Fulton Fish Market the same year, sent there by a Maryland commerical fisherman. Church's record may be broken before these words see print.

Charles Cinto's magnificent striper, incidentally, was not accepted by the International Game Fish Association for record recognition because it was taken on tackle not conforming to then-existing IGFA rules. Cinto's combination is said to have been a gang-hook plug draped with an eelskin, trolled on wire line along Sow and Pigs Reef, off Cuttyhunk Island.

While stripers as large as 125 pounds have been reported as having been taken in "the old days" by commercial nets, the average fish available to sportsmen now on either coast is a good deal smaller. Generally speaking, stripers under 40 pounds are caught by the literal thousands. Fish in the 40 to 50 pound class are recorded in the hundreds, while bass in the select 50- to 60 pound category may total several score. Fish over 60 pounds are rare, but frequent enough to whet the appetite of every true striper-lover.

Chesapeake Bay is the cornerstone of East Coast breeding areas and supports a large striped bass commercial fishery as well as a very active sport fishery.

On the Atlantic Coast, stripers range from northern Florida up into the Bay of Fundy and the St. Lawrence River in Canada. The mid-point of the Atlantic range and the focus of eastern striper reproduction lies in the Chesapeake and Delaware Bay complex. Here is generated the excess populations of older, larger fish that range the coast from Cape Hatteras to Nova Scotia and New Brunswick.

Stripers were introduced into Pacific waters in 1879, when 135 fingerlings survived the long, slow, transcontinental train trip, and again in 1882 when 300 fish were planted in San Francisco Bay. Since then, Pacific stripers have grown into a major natural marine resource. Since 1935 they have been strictly game fish in California, not to be bought or sold on the commerical market.

At present the Pacific range of stripers is from a little below San Francisco in central California to northern Oregon, with reports of occasional strays coming from as far north as Washington. The greatest concentration is in the San Francisco Bay region, with smaller runs of good fish in various of the northern California and Oregon rivers to the north.

There are a few scattered populations of stripers across the northern edge of the Gulf of Mexico, but here, where water temperatures are at the upper limits tole-

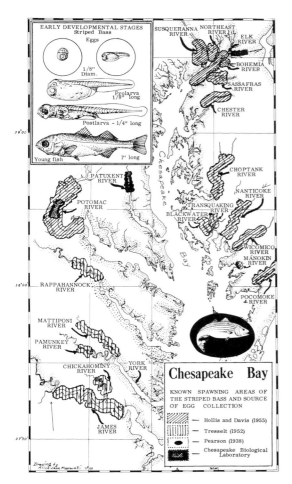

EARLY DEVELOPMENTAL STAGES
Striped Bass
Eggs

1/8"
Diam.

Prolarva
1/8" long

Postlarva – 1/4" long

Young fish   1" long

SUSQUEHANNA NORTHEAST
RIVER   RIVER   ELK
RIVER

BOHEMIA
RIVER

SASSAFRAS
RIVER

CHESTER
RIVER

PATUXENT
RIVER

POTOMAC
RIVER

CHOPTANK
RIVER

NANTICOKE
RIVER

TRANSQUAKING
RIVER
BLACKWATER
RIVER

WICOMICO
RIVER
MANOKIN
RIVER

RAPPAHANNOCK
RIVER

POCOMOKE
RIVER

MATTIPONI
RIVER

PAMUNKEY
RIVER

CHICKAHOMINY   YORK
RIVER   RIVER

Chesapeake Bay

KNOWN SPAWNING AREAS OF
THE STRIPED BASS AND SOURCE
OF EGG COLLECTION

— Hollis and Davis (1955)

— Tresselt (1952)

— Pearson (1938)

— Chesapeake Biological
Laboratory

JAMES
RIVER

Drawing by
Alice Jane Manwell: 1/00

Known Chesapeake spawning areas.

fish. But in a few rivers and lakes, there appear to be small, self-sustaining populations of fresh water stripers. This is explored in greater detail in the chapter on "Stripers in Fresh Water."

Let us turn now to the great breeding areas of the East and West for a closer look at what really makes *Roccus* run.

On the West Coast, the most important breeding area is the Sacramento-San Joaquin River delta region of San Francisco Bay. Other western rivers contribute small additions to the Pacific population. In the East, the prime producing region is the Pamlico Sound, Chesapeake Bay, Delaware Bay complex of the mid-Atlantic coast. Many rivers from Florida to Canada have smaller breeding populations that help to increase the total.

In most areas stripers breed in fresh water not more than 20 or 25 miles from the nominal dividing line between fresh water and salt. They are anadromous fish, meaning that they spend most of their adult lives in the sea, but ascend fresh water rivers to breed.

One outstanding exception to the general Chesapeake-Delaware coastal breeding pattern is the population of stripers that ascend the Roanoke River in North Carolina for more than 100 miles to find acceptable breeding areas. Many coastal rivers north of Delaware Bay sustain local breeding populations. Most of these populations are small and do not add significantly to the overall bulk of migratory stripers, but the Hudson River population, now recognized as a distinct subrace of *Roccus saxatilis*, is quite active and provides most of the stripers that are caught in western and central Long Island Sound.

Tagging by scientists and sportsmen has been extensive over the years and has been largely instrumental in determining the range and spread of various striper populations. Details of striper-tagging are discussed in other chapters.

rated by stripers, the populations are in part or almost totally brackish or fresh water in habitat.

In South Carolina, when the dams of the Santee-Cooper reservoir complex were completed, a small population of stripers was locked into this fresh water environment. Over the years this fresh water population has stabilized, breeding in rivers tributary to the lakes. Hatchery-bred striped bass, at the time of this writing, have been introduced into at least 27 states and several foreign countries.

In most fresh water locations the introduction and harvesting of striped bass is on a put-and-take basis, proper breeding conditions seldom being available to the

North Carolina fisheries workers Bob Ray and Mel Englehart net a female bass raised from fry to maturity in the Edenton, N.C., state hatchery ponds.

Suspended in a net sling, a big female is lowered gently into a holding tank where she will live until tests prove her eggs to be at the peak of ripeness.

Bob Pond (foreground) of Stripers Unlimited assists biologist in stripping ripe eggs from a female bass during an early spring egg-gathering effort.

Fertilized eggs are kept in glass beakers with a constant flow of fresh water. Eggs will sink to the bottom and suffocate if the flow stops in a beaker, or in a river.

Avis Boyd feeds brine shrimp to tiny bass fry at the Stripers Unlimited headquarters in South Attleboro, Mass., a center for restoring stripers to local rivers.

Young *Roccus* gets his start in life when gravid (pregnant) females and smaller, more numerous male stripers push up the rivers from the sea in the spring of the year. There is strong evidence that stripers are imprinted with the chemical identity of their natal streams and, in many cases, return to rivers of their birth.

Water temperature plays an important role in triggering the breeding act. Spawning takes place from early April in rivers of the extreme southern part of the range to June or July in New Brunswick, Canada, and mostly at temperatures between 58° and 70° F.

Research shows that individual females become fully ripe at different times during this season. There is a critical 60-minute period following ovulation during which eggs must be extruded if spawning is to be successful. Eggs retained by the female longer than the criti-

cal 60-minute period will be over-ripe and impossible to fertilize.

Spawning can be spectacular to watch. Nature arranges things so that each gravid female is accompanied by a number of smaller, more active males. When the hour of full ripeness comes, these males rub and thrust against the belly and flanks of the female in a whirling, splashing dance called a "rock-fight."

The term "rock-fight" refers to the fact that, from southern New Jersey to Texas, the striped bass is called the rockfish or rock. To say that the males are fighting with the female is incorrect. They are actually carrying out a nuptial act that stimulates her to extrude eggs. As the eggs are passed, the males also expend sperm-bearing milt. The water turns milky with the mixed sexual products.

The sheer mass of these products is amazing. A 50-pound female may extrude up to 5,000,000 eggs of which only a few individuals may be destined to survive to full adulthood. The eggs are short-lived and die if not fertilized within a few moments. The fertilized eggs are spherical, slightly greenish in color, and have a slight tendency to sink in fresh water.

Because of the vulnerability of the eggs to siltation and smothering on the bottom in non-moving water, most breeding takes place in rivers with definite current. The eggs "water harden" quickly after fertilization. Incubation is rapid, taking about 30 hours at water temperatures of 70° to 72° F, 48 hours at 64°, and 70 to 75 hours at between 58° and 60°.

The freshly hatched fry are minute creatures with only limited mobility. They do not feed until the yolk-sac, attached to the stomach, is fully absorbed. When this has happened, the fry become fully mobile and quickly start to feed on minute one-celled and multi-celled plant and animal life present in the water.

At this stage the striper fry are prime food for slightly larger fish, their own species included. Cannibalism is prevented to a large degree by the way fingerlings tend to move into deeper, more open waters of the estuarine regions, such as Chesapeake Bay, where they mature. At the end of the first year, the young are from two to five inches long and feed in small groups. As they grow larger they tend to gather in schools of larger size.

Maximum temperatures that permit stripers to survive appear to be between 80° and 86° F. Minimum temperatures for normal feeding and activity seem to be 44° to 46° F. Stripers wintering in coastal rivers where water temperatures fall below these values become lethargic and torpid, often submitting to netting or spearing—activities that would cause them to flee if the water were warmer.

Other than size, there is no way to determine the sex of a striper without opening the body cavity. Most very large individuals are female. The largest male I have been able to discover in research literature is a 40-pounder. A few individuals prove to be hermaphroditic, having both ovaries and testes present in the same fish. A consistant shift of sex from male to female, or vice versa, has not been established, however.

The growth of striped bass can be represented by a parabolic curve on a linear graph. The accompanying chart gives the approximate age and weight of a striper, the length of which is known. Both the solid weight line and the dashed age line are averages, taken from a number of fish of known dimensions and accurately estimated ages.

The growth display on page 16 by Alice Mansueti was taken from a report on striped bass by biologist Romeo Mansueti when he was working for the Maryland Department of Fisheries. It represents similar information in pictorial form.

In judging really big fish, some anglers work by the so-called 50-50 rule in which a 50-inch striper is considered to weigh just about 50-pounds. Because of the exponential nature of fish growth, a 60-inch striper will weigh a lot more than 60-pounds. Church's record 73-pounder was 60 inches long with a girth of 30½ inches.

For estimating the weight of big stripers, the following formula is fairly accurate (measurements in inches):

$$\text{Weight} = \frac{\text{Girth}^2 \times \text{Length}}{800}$$

A simpler formula with the same range of accuracy is :

$$\text{Weight} = \frac{\text{Girth} \times \text{Length}}{26}$$

Individual stripers vary in shape, depth of belly, fat content, sexual tissue content, and other weight-influencing characteristics. Fish of the same length or age may

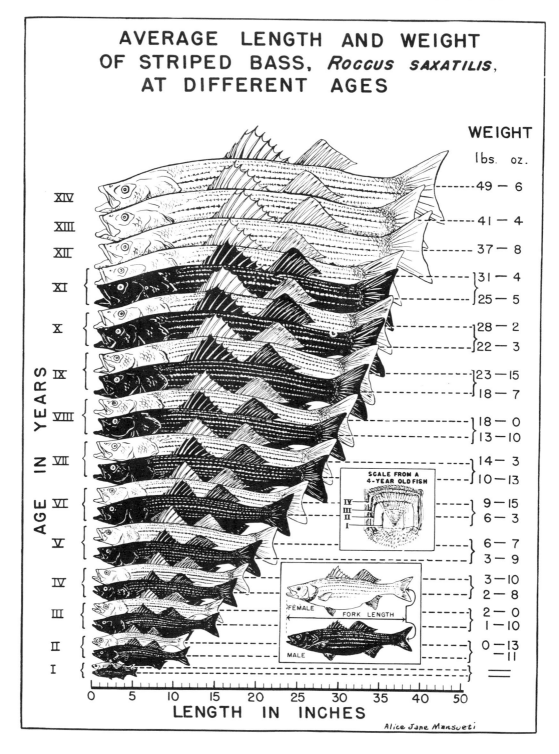

AVERAGE LENGTH AND WEIGHT OF STRIPED BASS, *Roccus saxatilis*, AT DIFFERENT AGES

differ from each other by a number of pounds. Age can be estimated in younger fish with a good degree of accuracy by counting scale-rings as you would count rings in a cross-section of a tree trunk.

It is the cyclic, migratory activity of stripers that makes them attractive to so many sportsmen. Here is a tribe of fish whose coming and going can be predicted with considerable accuracy over a broad pattern, yet which can be delightfully or exasperatingly unpredictable when it comes to specific locations and particular calendar dates in the future.

Until stripers reach the age of three or four years, they do not wander far from the estuaries of their juvenile growth. But as they become larger, requiring bigger, more active food, a cyclic wanderlust appears to goad them into extensive coastwise migrations.

In the Atlantic the main thrust of this migration is east and north from the Chesapeake region toward New England and the Canadian Maritime Provinces. In the Pacific it pushes north from central California toward Oregon, Washington, and possibly British Columbia. In both cases the summer ranks of migratory fish are swelled by unspecified, but not unimportant, numbers of stripers from localized populations in rivers and estuaries along the way.

While stripers have a strong instinct to school, they are often highly individualistic within the school. However, each school appears to have a spontaneous collective identity and, one might say, intelligence. Learning to predict what these fish will do under different circumstances shifts from mundane science to something that borders on the occult.

Bob Pond, founder of "Stripers Unlimited" and designer and manufacturer of the famous Atom line of plugs, expressed the dedicated striper fisherman's viewpoint when he said, "Seldom has any ocean spawned a more contrary, challenging fish. How do you catch stripers? First you must feel that your family will starve to death if you don't bring fish home for dinner.

"You must be willing to endure cold, dampness, lack of sleep, fatigue, and often pain without losing your powers of concentration and perception. Every sense must stay sharp. Believe it or not, stripers are fish that seem to remember experiences of pain and danger and appear able to pass this information to other fish of the school."

Pond cites instances from his own experience in which a newly developed plug or lure has been red-hot for a while, but after being continually used on the fish in the commerical quantities now afforded by mass production, the red-hot lure seems to cool off in its attractiveness to stripers, even though it continues to take a respectable share of fish.

Pond's statement, "First you must feel that your family will starve to death . . ." puts the finger of self-analysis squarely on the pscyhe of the dedicated bass fisherman. Some anglers feel this compelling drive more than others, but all successful striper fishermen have one trait in common—they take great pains to understand the striper in his environment.

From a fisherman's point of view, how do stripers behave in their environment?

The question is as broad as it is long, but we can start answering it by listing those phases of behavior that directly affect the fisherman's success. Pared to the essential points, the list looks like this:

1. The kinds of quantity of natural bait present.

2. Effect of tides and moon phases on the fish.

3. How fish respond to the geographical location.

4. The effect of past and present weather.

5. Competition from other species of fish.

6. The effect of human activities on the fish.

Let us examine each of these points briefly in turn, not trying to work out all the possible answers, but bringing each important point into focus so that, as we see them now and elsewhere in the book, we can expand the mental picture of each until we are able to fit together many parts of the striper jigsaw puzzle.

Natural bait. The most important single lesson a striper fisherman can learn is how to spot and recognize the important kinds of bait, striper food, in the water.

Sometimes you can do this directly, as when you spot gulls or terns feeding on sand eels or other small bait fish driven to the surface by larger fish down below. At other times you have to use indirect means, such as inspecting the stomach contents of freshly caught bass.

Spotting and recognizing the bait is just the beginning. Once you know what kind of bait is present, you must be able to interpret this information in terms of the lures, natural bait, and fishing tactics you will have to use to catch the fish.

Tides and moon phases. Intimately related to bass is the life-pulse of the sea, the ebb and flow of the tides. Fish in fresh water live a 24-hour day, reacting to the daily cycle of sunlight and darkness, warmth and coolness. But stripers in salt water are governed by a 25-hour day dictated by the swing of the moon in its orbit around the earth and the effect of the moon's gravity on the rise and fall of the tides.

Mention moon phases to a fresh water fisherman and he invariably thinks in terms of a popular type of sun-moon time table that is supposed to show major and minor "periods of activity" during which fish and wild game reputedly move out of shelter seeking food. But mention moon phases to a striper fisherman and his reaction is to think of whether the moon will be full, new, on the wax or on the wane, at its apogee (farthest away position in orbit), or at perigee (closest to the earth in orbit).

All of this important moon information, including the time of high and low slack water and maximum ebb and flood tides at many given points along our coasts, is contained in two important books, the *Tide Tables* and *Tidal Current Tables* published by the U.S. Department of Commerce and available at most marine chart and nautical supply stores.

When tides flow ebb or flood, stripers move about seeking food, exploring new territory, or schooling together in answer to natural urges. During high and low water slack current periods, stripers become retiring, not easily interested in food or lures, suspicious of every unnatural noise or movement in the water.

Learn how the stripers in your area react to tidal currents and the phases of the moon and you will be able to predict in advance when fishing conditions will be promising, provided the weather cooperates.

Stripers act differently in different geographical areas. For example, when stripers first appear in the spring in coastal bays and estuaries they move into the shallow bay channels on the rising tide seeking the shrimp and marine worms that are plentiful there. At this time, fishing with a salt water fly rod or a light spinning outfit and artificial lures imitating shrimp or worms will take the fish.

But when these same fish leave the bays for the open water of large sounds and the ocean, the food and fishing techniques that interested them inside no longer attract their attention.

Each locality seems to have fishing methods that work well season after season. Their success is due to the way the successful baits or lures fit into the striper's behavioral pattern in combination with the tides, natural food, and location.

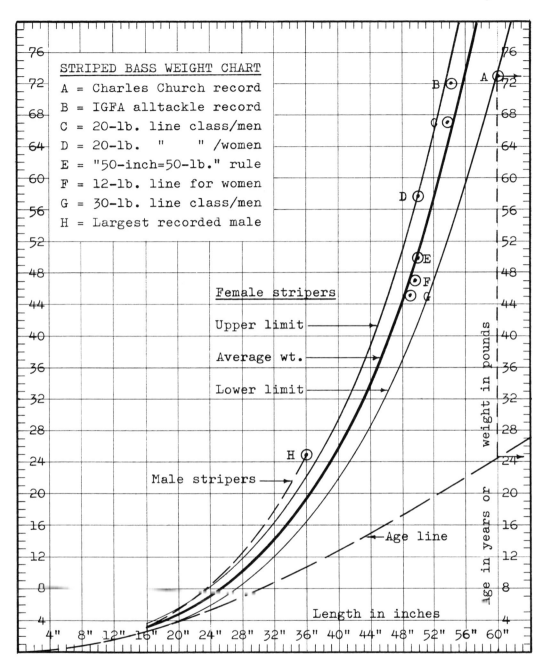

STRIPED BASS WEIGHT CHART
A = Charles Church record
B = IGFA alltackle record
C = 20-lb. line class/men
D = 20-lb. "   " /women
E = "50-inch=50-lb." rule
F = 12-lb. line for women
G = 30-lb. line class/men
H = Largest recorded male

Female stripers

Upper limit

Average wt.

Lower limit

Male stripers

Age line

Length in inches

weight in pounds

age in years or

To read your striper's approximate weight, find its length at bottom of chart, then look up the vertical length line to where it crosses the average weight line. Stripers vary in build, so upper and lower weight limits are given. The approximate age can also be read by finding the point where the length line crosses the dashed age line, then reading from the right-hand vertical scale. For example, Charles Church's 73-pounder measured 60 inches long and was about 24½ years old.

Weather plays a big part. People who don't understand stripers invariably equate a sunny, mild day with good fishing weather. But stripers love rough weather with surf, waves, and churning tides. They're wet already so rain doesn't bother them. Some of the best fishing takes place during weather that landlubbers wouldn't call fit for a polar bear.

As a broad rule, stripers are most active during spells of falling or low barometer, under overcast skies, during moderately rough conditions, and when there is a definite bloom of "color" or sediment in the water.

They are inclined to be least active on a sharply rising barometer after a storm, during the clear, calm weather of a prolonged barometric "high," and when water is extremely clean, clear, and without surf.

But they are perverse enough to change in the face of the most experienced advice, "blitzing" when the so-called smart fishermen are sleeping out a slow tide and giving the chumps who are lucky enough to cash in on such a blitz reason to boast, "Hell, these fish aren't so tough!"

Later on they find out the truth, but this is how a lot of striper fishermen are recruited.

Competition from other species. During the long, hot summer months, competition from other aggressive species,

Nova Scotia guide Bob Miller affixes a tag to the tail of a school striper caught in southern Nova Scotia waters during a Sportfishing *Magazine research effort.*

bluefish especially, may put stripers definitely off their regular behavior. But during the fall migratory runs bluefish, pollock, mackerel, bonito, and even salmon on the Pacific Coast may appear feeding on the same schools of bait along with stripers.

Human activities. What people do on the water affects stripers in many ways. A handful of trolling or casting boats moving slowly over or through feeding bass seldom will spook them, but one or two fast boats zipping by at full speed will definitely put them down.

Amazingly, stripers seem able to adapt to boat activity. Witness the melee of boats and bass that often converge on such great trolling hot-spots as Montauk Point, Sandy Hook, the Chesapeake Bay Bridge, or in the delta region of San Francisco Bay.

Human activities affect the fish in other ways. Pollution takes heavy toll of eggs, larvae, and juvenile fish. Dredging of coastal bays and rivers destroys many nursery grounds of fingerling bass. Damming of coastal rivers takes breeding locations out of production.

On the reverse side of the human factor coin, biologists are making great strides in learning how to raise healthy striped bass fry and fingerlings in state hatcheries. The exciting story of how breakthroughs in this scientific field have been made is told in the chapter, "Stripers Invade Fresh Water."

It is not hard to see that there is no easy answer to the question, "What makes *Roccus* run?"

The dedicated striper fisherman lives through fatigue, frustration, and frequent self-doubt, so that he may occasionally savor the moments of supreme satisfaction that come when he has successfully outwitted these wild self-willed fish in their own element.

In the end he discovers that what makes *Roccus* run makes him run, also.

3 / Tackle for Stripers

WHILE SPECIFIC TACKLE RECOMMENDATIONS are given quite liberally throughout this book, readers may find it convenient to refer to the following condensed tables of tackle recommended for various types of striper fishing. If there are slight differences between these tables and tackle recommended elsewhere for specific methods of fishing, please remember that the choice and selection of proper tackle is a relative matter, and no set of recommendations can be considered absolute.

For the sake of complete understanding, here are a few definitions of phrases used in the tables:

Heavy action in a rod means not a heavy rod tip in weight, but a rod tip designed to have plenty of stiffness and backbone for the line it is to work with. Rods should be chosen to match the class of line recommended. You can have "heavy," "medium," and "light" or "soft" action in three different rods, all designed to handle the same basic line.

Medium action as its name implies denotes a grade of stiffness or backbone halfway between the extremes of heavy and light or soft. It is the most commonly used by anglers, and should be selected if a rod in either heavy or light action is not available.

Light or *soft action* refers to a rod with maximum flexibility without being spongy in response to stress. It is usually specified in instances when the angler needs the greatest amount of elasticity between himself and the fish. It is almost always used with wire line because wire has no built-in stretch factor, therefore the rod alone must absorb all of the sudden stress of a heavy strike.

In selecting line where either Dacron or mono is recommended, remember that mono has more stretch than Dacron. If your rod is definitely "soft," you should select Dacron line where a choice is indicated. On the other hand, if your rod happens to be rather stiff for the type of fishing involved, mono line will add the extra flexibility your tackle combination may require.

Surface trolling, heavy duty (fish over 30 lb.):
Rod   —6½' heavy action, trolling.
Reel   —Penn 4/0 #114H, or equal.
Line   —50 lb. test Dacron or mono.
Backing —none
Leader   —80 lb. test mono.
Hooks   —6/0 to 8/0, various models.

Surface trolling, light duty (fish under 30 lb.):
Rod   —5½' medium action, trolling.
Reel   —Penn 3/0 #113H or equal.
Line   —30 lb. test Dacron or mono.
Backing —none
Leader   —50 lb. test mono.
Hooks   —3/0 to 5/0, various models.

Deep trolling, heavy duty (fish over 30 lb.):
Rod   —6½' medium to soft action, trolling.
Reel   —Penn 4/0 #114H or equal.
Line   —.024″ (45 lb. test) soft-drawn Monel.
Backing —50 lb. test Dacron or mono.
Leader   —80 lb. test mono.

A good rod, a faithful reel, a gaff, and a selection of plugs and metals—these are really all that a striper fisherman needs to take bass from the beach.

Hooks   —6/0 to 8/0, various models.

Deep trolling, light duty (fish under 30 lb.):

Rod   —5½' soft action, trolling.

Reel   —Penn Jigmaster #500M or equal.

Line   —.018″ (25 lb. test) soft-drawn Monel.

Backing —30–36 lb. test Dacron or mono.

Leader —40 lb. test mono.

Hooks   —3/0 to 5/0, various models.

Bucktail jigging (fish to 30 lb.):

Rod   —7½' medium to heavy action, jigging.

Reel   —Penn Jigmaster #500M or equal.

Line   —30 lb. test mono.

Backing —none

Leader —none, or 40 lb. test mono.

Hooks   —2/0 to 5/0, various models.

Drifting sea worms (fish up to 20 lb.):

Rod   —7½' medium action, jigging or casting.

Reel   —Penn Squidder #145 or equal.

Line   —20 lb. test mono.

Backing —none

Leader —none

Hooks   —1/0 to 3/0 Eagle Claw bait-holder model.

Live bait, heavy duty (fish over 30 lb.):

Rod   —7½' heavy action, jigging or casting.

Reel   —Penn Jigmaster #500M or equal.

Line   —20–30 lb. test mono.

Backing —none

Leader —none

Hooks   —4/6 to 6/0 various models.

Live bait, light duty (fish under 30 lb.):

Rod   —7½' medium action, jigging or casting.

Reel   —Penn Squidder #145 or equal.

Line   —15–20 lb. test mono.

Backing —none

Leader —none

Rhode Island fishing guide Al Anderson finds spinning tackle ideal for his specialty, light tackle plugging for bass from a fast 19-foot Aquasport.

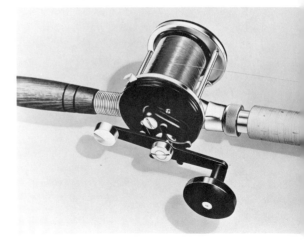

The Garcia Ambassadeur 10,000C revolving spool reel is an excellent model for casting or trolling with monofilament lines in the 30-pound line-test range.

Hooks —2/0 to 4/0, various models.

Surf casting, "Hatteras Heaver" ("conventional" reel):

Rod —10½' heavy action "conventional."

Reel —Penn Squidder #145 or equal.

Line —30–36 lb. test casting Dacron.

Backing —none

Leader —40 lb. test mono.

Hooks —4/0 to 8/0, various models.

Surf casting, "Hatteras Heaver" (spinning):

Rod —11' heavy action spinning.

Reel —Penn #704 or equal.

Line —20–30 lb. test mono.

Backing —none

Leader —30–40 lb. test mono.

Hooks —4/0 to 8/0, various models.

Surf casting, medium duty (fish 15 to 30 lb.):

Rod —9½' medium action spinning.

Reel —Penn #704 or equal.

Line —12–18 lbs. test mono.

Backing —none

Leader —none, or 4' of 30–40 lb. test mono.

Hooks —3/0 to 6/0, various models.

Surf casting, light duty (fish under 15 lb.):

Rod —8' light spinning.

Reel —Penn #712, Cardinal, or equal.

Line —8–12 lb. test mono.

Backing —none

Leader —none, or 3' of 20–30 lbs. test mono.

Hooks —1/0 to 4/0, various models.

Ultra-light casting, surf or boat:

Rod —7' light action, spinning.

Reel —Any good, small spinning reel.

Line —6 lb. test tournament mono.

Backing —none

Leader —none, or 3' of 20 lb. test mono.

Hooks —1/0 to 3/0, various models.

Fresh water bait-casting tackle (fish up to 30 lb.):

Rod —Any heavy duty bait-casting model.

Reel —Any heavy duty bait-casting model.

Line —20 lb. test braided or mono.

Backing —none

Leader —30 lb. test mono.

Hooks —2/0 to 4/0, various models.

Fly fishing, heavy duty (fish over 20 lb.):

Rod —9'–9½' matching Weight 9 casting line.

Reel —Fin-Nor #2 or equal.

Line —WF-9-F/S (weight forward, sinking tip).

Backing —30 lb. test Dacron or mono.
Leader   —(see chapter on fly casting).
Hooks   —#2 to 4/0, various models.
Fly fishing, light duty (fish under 20 lb.):
Rod   —7½'–8½' matching Weight 7
          casting line.
Reel   —Scientific Anglers System 7
          or equal.
Line   —WF-7-S (weight forward,
          sinking).
Backing —20 lb. test Dacron or mono.
Leader   —(see chapter on fly casting).
Hooks   —#4 to 2/0, various models.

Spinning tackle is almost universally used for many types of striper fishing, and it is useful to look at the five classes of tackle commonly used. Remember that here we are judging spinning tackle against striped bass, and what may be light to medium spinning tackle to some other anglers can be classed as ultra-light with these robust fish. By sticking close to the line diameters, line tests, and lure weights recommended, an angler is assured of balanced tackle that will perform well under the conditions for which it was built.

Remember that not all monofilament lines have the same diameter for the same breaking strain, and you may encounter diameters and breaking tests that will vary slightly from the figures given here. Smart anglers provide at least one

and often two extra spools for each reel. The spools are filled with lines of slightly different diameters, spanning the line-test range for each class of spinning tackle. If you do this, mark each spool with the breaking strain of the line it contains.

By definition, nylon is any long-chain synthetic polymeric amide with recurring amide groups as an integral part of the main polymer chain. It is capable of being extruded and solidified under slight tension, then stretched, during which process the molecular elements of the filament are oriented in the direction of the axis. Nylon monofilament has a tensile strength of from 70,000 to 100,000 pounds per square inch of cross section, depending on type. This is about the strength of mild steel wire.

Nylon filaments elongate 15 to 30 percent when dry and 20 to 35 percent when wet before breaking. This is one reason why "heavy" or "stiff" action rods are often suggested for use with monofilament. The specific gravity of nylon ranges from 1.08 to 1.15, and nylon will absorb from three to ten percent of its weight of water. Water absorption usually entails a slight loss of tensile strength, seldom over ten percent.

Dacron is a trade mark for a duPont polyester fiber manufactured in much the same manner as nylon. Most Dacron lines

Comparative Tackle Table

Rod class	Average line dia.	Line test	Lure weight
Ultra-light	.008″	4 lb.	1/4 oz.
	.009″–.010″	5 lb.	3/8 oz.
	.010″–.011″	6 lb.	1/2 oz.
Light	.011″–.012″	7 lb.	3/8–5/8 oz.
	.013″	8 lb.	1/2–3/4 oz.
Medium	.015″	10 lb.	1/2–1 oz.
	.018″	14 lb.	1–2 oz.
Heavy	.021″	17 lb.	1–3 oz.
	.026″	25 lb.	2–4 oz.
Extra-heavy	.028″	30 lb.	3–5 oz.

Comparative Leader Table

Leader test	Wire size	Wire diameter	Mono diameter
20 lb.			.024″
25 lb.			.026″
30 lb.			.028″
40 lb.	#4	.013″	.032″
50 lb.	#5	.014″	.036″
60 lb.	#6	.016″	.040″
80 lb.	#7	.018″	.048″

are braided and the strength of Dacron is about equal to that of nylon. Dacron has less stretch, however, usually not over ten percent. Most of Dacron's stretch occurs just before breaking, while nylon stretches throughout its full working range. Dacron is less affected by sunlight and water and has about the same specific gravity and sinking ability as nylon.

Leaders for striped bass lures are made up from both monofilament and stainless steel wire with mono preferred in the lower half of the leader-test range. The above table gives comparative data for the seven classes of leaders most commonly used by striper anglers.

Hooks are extremely important to any fishing operation and the proper choice of style and size can have considerable influence on fishing success. Most striped bass anglers stick to just a few well-known hook styles, but do not hesitate to change hook sizes to suit the size of the fish, the size and weight of the lure or bait, and other variable conditions. The most frequently-used hook styles are as follows.

O'Shaughnessy. This is widely used in sizes from 2/0 to 8/0 for rigging trolling lures. The point is medium long, straight, and has a moderate barb. The sides of the wire at the shank and bend of the hook are rolled flat for greater strength against bending and breaking. The hook is usually tinned against corrosion. It is obtainable in ringed or needle eye; the latter is favored for rigging eels. It is usually sold unsnelled.

Sproat. This superficially resembles the O'Shaughnessy in shape, but with a slightly shallower bend and generally smaller wire diameter for "O" size. The sides are not rolled. It is popular in smaller sizes for rigging worm rigs and other bait-fishing rigs for small- to medium-sized stripers. It is often sold snelled, but obtainable unsnelled.

Eagle Claw. This is a trademarked hook style manufactured by the Wright & McGill Company. It features a very sharp, fast, slightly curved point with good barb, and is widely used for live bait fishing and for rigging small- to medium-sized trolling and some casting lures.

Sobey. This heavy-duty, big game style of hook is sometimes used in the smaller sizes from 2/0 to 6/0 for rigging large metal spoons. Twin Sobey hooks of 10/0 size are occasionally rigged back-to-back, ice-tongs fashion, to a single large split ring in the tail of a bunker spoon. The Sobey has a heavy wire diameter with a machine-ground, slightly hollow point. It is very strong, but quite heavy for the "O" size.

Treble or gang hooks. These are very widely used in sizes of #4 to about 4/0 as body and tail hooks in casting plugs. They are also frequently used with live mackerel or herring. IGFA tackle rules now permit the use of not more than two treble hooks in plugs designed to be used for casting. Their use in trolling is not sanctioned by IGFA tackle rules.

Important auxiliary equipment found

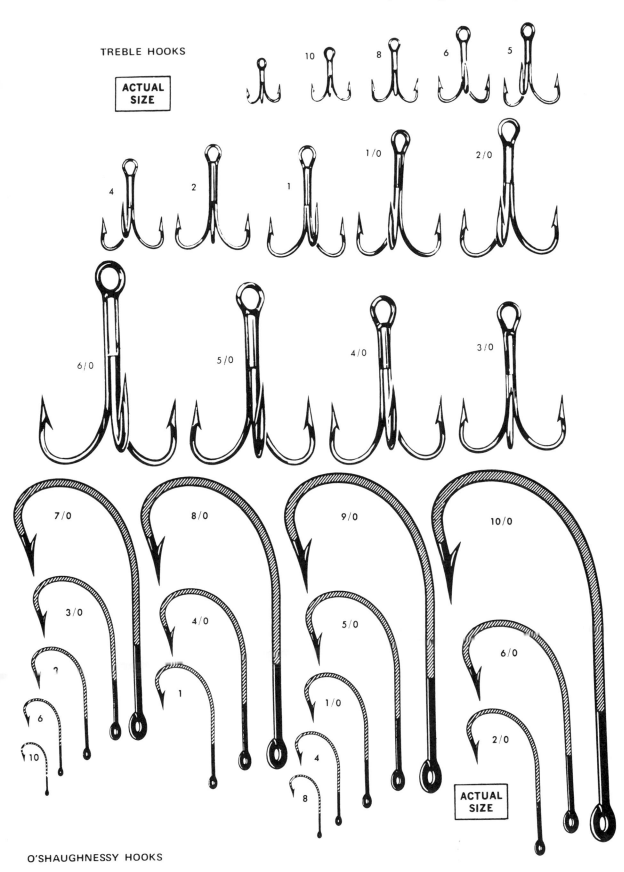

TREBLE HOOKS

ACTUAL SIZE

O'SHAUGHNESSY HOOKS

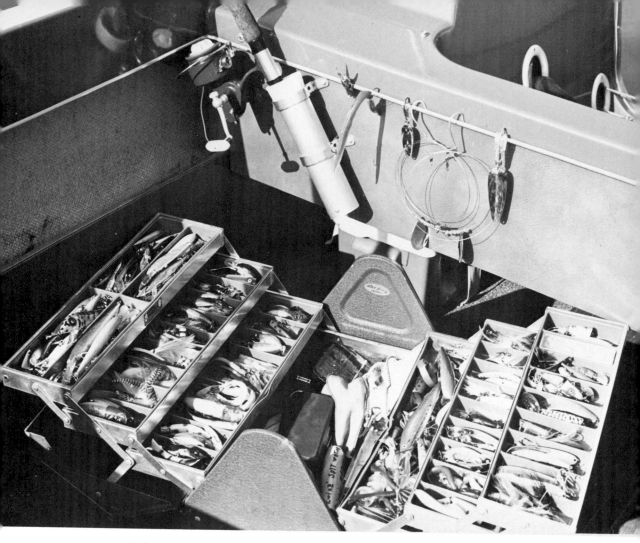

What every well-stocked striper fisherman should have, if he can afford it.

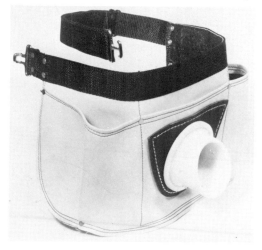

A rod apron with pockets is a big help.

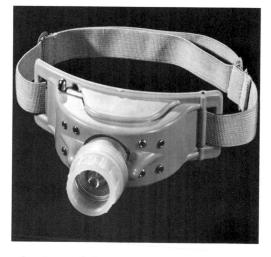

So is a fisherman's adjustable head lamp.

in every striper fisherman's tackle box, whether he fishes from the surf or a boat, include the following items:

- Parallel-jaw rigging pliers
- Bait-cutting knife
- Assorted bait-fishing and trolling sinkers
- Wire and monofilament leader material
- Assorted swivels and connectors
- Leader sleeve crimping pliers
- Oil stones for knives and hooks
- Reel wrenches and repair kit
- Spray and gear lubricant
- Assorted stainless steel split rings
- Plastic electrician's tape
- De-liar weight scale and tape measure
- Assorted pork rind in jars.
- Plug and lure-head touch-up lacquer
- Welding-rod eel-rigging needle
- Heavy cotton eel-rigging twine
- Dispenser of dental floss
- Unrigged feather heads and eel bobs
- Rigged eel action heads
- Unrigged bucktail treble hooks
- Surfman's short hand gaff
- Miner's night light and batteries
- Plastic live-bait fishing line
- Spare wire and soft fishing line
- Spare plugs, jigs, lures as needed
- Band Aides and mercurochrome
- Small flask of snake bite remedy

While a complete home workshop is not within the capability of every fisherman, most dedicated striper men find places at home for adequate storage space for their rods, reels, tackle boxes, waders, and other equipment. Some anglers take pride in manufacturing much of their essential equipment, going to the extremes of putting together and winding their own rods, molding sinkers and casting jigs, and rigging and painting casting and trolling lures.

Whether you are a do-it-yourselfer or a person whose other commitments preclude spending much time in a home workshop, the final great secret of success with stripers is to keep your equipment in good shape, stocking those particular items that give multiple service. When you go out fishing, plan ahead what equipment to take that will answer the needs of the place, time, and season. Don't overload with useless stuff just because you own it.

Finally, avoid the habit of equating fishing fun with dollars spent. This is a landlubber trick that obscures the true joy of fishing. Don't be ashamed to bring fish home to eat or to give to friends, but kill and bring home only those fish for which you have actual use. Tag and release the excess and your fishing will take on new meaning when, eventually, you experience the rare thrill of getting one of your tags back.

The Dyercraft 29, built of fiberglass by The Anchorage of Warren, R.I., is typical of the modern trend in fast, functional, good-looking bass boats.

4 / Boats for Stripers

THE TERM "STRIPED BASS BOAT" HAS BECOME synonymous with seaworthiness, agility, and functional planning in a specialized class of powerboats. The boats that are now used for striped bass fishing have interesting antecedents.

Back before World War II, a boat designed specifically for the pursuit of this single species was a pretty radical idea. Those of us who fished for stripers with charter boats or small commerical craft made do with converted cabin cruisers, small lobster boats, or even flat-bottomed fish trap sharpies with a Model A motor chugging under a box in the middle.

One non-professional fisherman at Montauk consistently out-produced all but the most diligent professionals. His name was Otto Scheer and he had brought engineering training to the problem of creating a boat capable of trolling in the ocean surf. His *Punkinseed* was like no other boat most of us had ever seen.

Hardly 20 feet long, she was a wide, shallow double-ender with what was probably the very first center console for steering and motor controls. Her single rudder and propeller were protected by a heavy skeg, yet she was cat-quick in response to wheel or throttle.

Otto Scheer's boon companion and trusted skipper was the appropriately named Bill Bassett. Together in *Punkinseed*, they drove the rest of us up the wall, trolling blithely among rocks and behind surf-roaring bars where we feared for our lives to follow.

Writing about Scheer and Bassett in his classic book *Salt Water Fishing*, the late Van Campen Heilner said that when his time came to cross the River Styx, he expected to find not Charon but Bill Bassett at the helm of *Punkinseed*, with Otto Scheer in the bow looking for rocks and urging, "Watch her, Bill. Now ease her in a bit."

At about the time that Otto Scheer was taking his census of the Montauk rocks, down Cuttyhunk-way a different kind of bass boat was evolving. The Cuttyhunk fishermen trolled a lot, but they also liked to cast from their boats into the rips and close to the rock ledges that stud the waters of the Elizabeth Islands and Martha's Vinyard.

The boat they developed was an open, V-bottomed, square-sterned power skiff not much over 22 feet long. Some Cuttyhunk bass boats were smooth-planked from keel to sheer-strake. Others were smooth on the bottom, but lapstrake above the chine. All were heavily built and had skegs to protect the single rudder and propeller. They depended on weight and the strong righting moment of their hard-chined hulls for stability in rough water.

The Cuttyhunkers were not as fast as many other craft of the same size and power, but, like their cousins the Maine lobster boats, they had, and still have, an amazing ability to slice along through nasty going with a minimum of fuss and pounding.

New Jersey fishermen of the same era

This 30-foot wooden Cuttyhunker built by the Mackenzie Boat Company exemplifies the strong, fast, seaworthy model developed to fish the rips of Cuttyhunk Island.

used the famous Jersey sea skiff, Sea-Bright dory, or "Jersey-boat" for their 'longshore bass fishing. The original Jersey sea skiff was a lightweight, completely open, lapstrake hull of moderate beam, usually between 18 feet and 30 feet long. The engine was under a box amidships and the shaft extended aft through a tapered, open, plank-box keel.

The box keel gave the bottom of the boat a flat, narrow, double-ended surface that facilitated launching or retrieving the boat directly from an ocean beach. Each Jersey-boat carried an iron ring in the stem to which a team of horses could be hitched. With a willing team, some rollers, and a man or two to help, a sea skiff with a half-ton of fresh fish in her could be snaked up above high water mark in just a few puffs of a corncob pipe.

In considering any complicated problem, it pays to use what engineers call the systems approach. There are three ways this approach can be applied to the choice of one's personal bass boat.

First, there are three major techniques for catching stripers from boats; casting,

trolling, and bait fishing. The first two have had the greatest influence on boat design and equipment selection.

Second, cutting across the grain of these three techniques are several types of boat uses that help to narrow a man's choice. These include: using very small boats for launching directly from a beach, boats that are transported by car-top or light trailer; using slightly larger high speed outboard boats with trailers for mobility over wide geographical areas; using specialized bass boats such as the Cuttyhunker for special trolling or casting situations; using full-sized sport fishing cruisers for open-water trolling with charter or private parties.

Third, there is the would-be angler's personal background. Are you a striper fisherman of some experience who is looking for a more sharply refined fishing machine? Are you primarily a boatman who sees in striped bass a challenging new way to extend your experience and enjoyment on the water? Or are you a duffer who is looking for his first real boat and envisions fishing for stripers because

Jean Two of Montauk is a charter boat type that has proven extremely popular at many important sport fishing ports along the Atlantic coast.

Boats like this 14-foot metal Aluma-Craft are popular with striper fishermen who tow their lightweight outboards on trailers behind Jeeps or camper trucks.

The fiberglass, twin-outboard, Florida-built Robalo, is at home in northern striped bass waters.

A 17-foot Boston Whaler in its element off a shoreside mansion at Newport, R.I.

they are available, good to eat, and represent to you the most logical major salt water game on which to spend your efforts? Whatever your viewpoint, keep it in mind as we go through the classes of boats that modern striper fishermen are using.

The small portables. These average 10 feet to 15 feet long, are portable by car-top carrier or light trailer, and are made primarily of aluminum for lightness, although there are a number of fiberglass models. Used primarily by surf casters, the light portables have extended the operating range of shore fishermen far beyond their normal casting distance from shore.

These are essentially two-man boats powered with small outboard motors of from 10 to 40 horsepower. Their great advantage lies in the fact that they can be transported overland to a scene of action and then launched directly from the beach. Their small size restricts them to casting, light trolling, and live-bait fishing in protected waters.

The small portables make up in land mobility what they lack in water cruising range and rough water capability. Hulls cost from a few hundred dollars to a top of about $1,000. Outboard motors in the 10 to 40 horsepower range average (at the time of this writing) about $20 per horsepower of power rating. Useful adjuncts are portable "lunch box" electronic sounders and Citizens Band walkie-talkie units for communicating with other boats or the angler's shore-based recreation vehicle.

Limitations of these boats are short operating range and duration, relatively low speed, small load capacity, and the need for good weather and moderate surf for launching, fishing, and retrieving.

The big portables. In the 16-foot to 26-foot class, these are are the outboard and inboard/outboard-powered fishing machines that have revolutionized sport fishing in many areas, striped bass fishing included. Fiberglass construction is the standard in a type of service where hand-lifting of the hull is seldom required. Hull forms favor the V-bottom or multi-chine styles, and most models are able to handle surprisingly rough water.

Passenger capacity ranges from two persons in the smallest models to six or more in the largest. Only the smallest can be beach-launched. The larger boats require hard-surfaced launching ramps in protected waters.

Power options range from a single 40 horsepower outboard up to twin 135-horsepower motors. Some I/O models feature one or two engines of up to 200 horsepower. Speeds are in proportion to power, with 35 to 40 knots not uncommon in many models. Depending on the fuel supply carried, operational range may extend to about 100 miles in outboard models, up to 200 miles in I/O models powered by four-cycle gasoline or diesel motors.

Almost all of the big portables feature the center control console and the raised forward casting deck. A few models in the largest sizes have an enclosed cuddy under the forward deck. Only the larger models sport toilet facilities. Many builders offer outriggers, fishing chairs, built-in fish and bait lockers, rod racks, and tackle lockers as part of the deal.

Beam is usually generous, with boats up to 24 feet in length usually built to comply with the eight-foot width rule for highway trailers now effective in most states. With their efficient design and layout, these boats are equally adaptable to trolling, casting, or bait fishing.

Trailers and towing vehicles give them the long-range mobility that they lack when on the water. Initial cost ranges from around $1,000 for the smallest models to as much as $8,000 for larger, deluxe models. A rule of the thumb for cost is that boats of this class cost approximately $2 per pound of weight, retail price. Many builders take special pains to provide adequate, protected space for installing elec-

This jet-driven, flat-bottomed Oregon Cape Kawanda Dory looks like a natural for striper fishing wherever there is surf and a good deal of shallow water.

tronic aids such as CB radios, sounders, water temperature gauges, RDF units, and fuel and battery condition meters.

Outboard or I/O power units average around $18 to $25 per rated horsepower. The weight of larger models may come close to weights of small house trailers, so transport trailers must be carefully chosen. Trailers cost from a low of around $400 for light-capacity models to well over $2,000 for units capable of handling the biggest portables.

In action the big portables approach the Cuttyhunker or other true bass boat types in fishing efficiency. Stability is usually very good and they are very agile. They are comfortable for experienced fishermen who don't need yacht-like accommodations, and they are easy to maintain.

Drawbacks are lack of cruising facilities and the relatively short water range imposed by a moderate fuel supply. Protection from wet weather is provided in some models by folding canvas spray tops. In others, the anglers have to make

do with foul-weather clothing. But these drawbacks are considered minor by the thousands of satisfied fishermen who have bought these boats for striped bass fishing and for other water pursuits.

The true bass boats. Of the designs discussed in the opening of this chapter, only the Cuttyhunk bass boat has survived to the present day in virtually unchanged form. Other types of inboard boats designed for striped bass fishing show a strong tendency to copy the Cuttyhunker in hull form and layout. The term "Cuttyhunker," incidentally, is a generic one and does not define the product of any single builder except as some builders have adopted the word into their model names.

Modern Cuttyhunkers retain the traditional sharp deadrise, hard-chine hull and average not much over 30 feet long. At least one builder uses a conventional lapstrake type of planking on the sides, but a reversed-lap bottom. The reversed-lap bottom has the overlap of the strakes

On the Chebogue River in southern Nova Scotia, Jerry Dominy from Long Island, N.Y., used this tiny Avon inflatable to good effect against Bluenose stripers.

running upward rather than downward like the shingles of a house roof.

Other builders utilize smooth planking, or a combination of lapstrake on the sides and smooth planking on the bottom. An increasing number of true bass boats are being built of fiberglass. The difference of material does not seem to detract from the boats' performance.

Configuration of the modern bass boat includes a long, open cockpit. The motor in smaller models is under a motor box, but in larger models may be under a slightly raised engine deck amidships. Forward, there is a small cuddy cabin with one or two bunks, a head, and in some models provision for a tiny galley. There is usually an open windshield with provision in many models for a folding canvas weather top.

The steering station at the stern features a folding tiller. Clutch and throttle controls are within easy reach. The forward steering station is now usually equipped with a conventional wheel. Rod holders are placed strategically for holding trolling rods or rods not used for casting. A few Cuttyhunkers have been equipped with small towers, lifting them out of the true bass boat category.

Twin-screw installations are now available, although many experienced bass experts prefer a good single-screw boat because of the protection to rudder and propeller afforded by the single-screw boat's skeg. Construction, especially in keel timbers, bottom frame and floor timbers, and bottom planking is usually substantial. As all experienced striped bass fishermen who fish from boats know, intimate knowledge of the locations of rocks is pounded into one's memory via the bottom of the boat.

Speed for a representative 29-foot fiberglass bass boat of modern design is quoted at about 17 knots with a 160-horsepower diesel and somewhat over 24 knots with a gasoline motor of around 250 horsepower. This may seem slow when compared with the performance of some more lightly built powerboats of equal power and size, but weight in a Cuttyhunker is a function of safety and stability in rough water.

Compared with lighter boats of the same size, the Cuttyhunker-style of boat may seem to be expensive, but on a dollar-per-pound cost basis, it averages the same as for most other power craft of the same size. Interestingly, some non-fishermen or occasional fishermen have found the Cuttyhunker to be an excellent day-sailing boat for family fun on the water and for moderate coastal cruising.

Where land portability is not a decisive factor, few boat types can beat the modern true bass boat for top performance in 'longshore casting and trolling, or in deep water exploratory trolling or bait fishing. Range is usually in excess of 200 miles, with fuel capacity equal to or not over 50 percent larger than that of the larger outboard-powered trailable boats.

Day-sailing capacity of the Cuttyhunk-style boat is at least six persons. Space for cruising accommodations is minimal, but for fishermen who demand boat performance over luxury, the Cuttyhunker is a very logical choice.

Larger sport fishing cruisers. Most offshore sport-fishing cruisers make excellent striped bass trolling boats where the fish are found in open-water conditions. The upper limit of practicality seems to be about 50-feet in length, although larger craft that are properly handled catch their share of the fish in deep water.

The size, draft, and value of the bigger boats make them basically unsuitable for close work in shallow water, except under special conditions that are discussed in other chapters. But in open water, especially in poor weather, the big boats make excellent striper-fishing machines.

A boat designed specifically for striped bass fishing is a great asset. But any well-laid-out fishing boat will catch stripers if it is used under the conditions that take advantage of its qualities. Matching the boat to conditions in your area will assure success.

One mistake that a great many landlubbers make is that they fail to distinguish between the boat-loving yachtsman and the boat-using fisherman. To the former the mere possession of a boat, like the owning of a good saddle horse to a horse-lover, is an end in itself.

But to the fisherman the boat is a means to an end, the fishing. Striper fishermen, especially, regard their boats in much the same light that the working cowpoke regards his horse—a tough, dependable ally able to perform regardless of the passage of time or the rough usage of their trade.

5 / Small Boat Safety

LAUNCHING AND LANDING A SMALL BOAT through the surf is great sport on a nice summer day, especially if there are fish a little way offshore to add spice to the venture. But every year inexperienced anglers, and a few experts too, get themselves into serious trouble on the water because they don't use common sense in mixing small boats and rough water.

Men and women who regularly take small power or rowing boats out through the surf for fishing recognize one cardinal rule. *If it looks too rough for you, it is too rough.* No genuine fisherman ever laughs at another who declines to tempt fate in a surf condtion that is too much for his skill.

But a little ordinary rough water doesn't keep many really good small boat striper fishermen from launching or beaching their boats when the fish are biting. The important thing is to know exactly how much surf you and your boat, and your fishing buddy, can handle. Launching is done sometimes with an inflated canvas beach-roller, sometimes "barefoot". In either case it goes this way:

The boat is brought to the water's edge and loaded with the fishing gear, etc. The motor is checked and tested, but left tilted up until the boat is actually afloat. The oars are shipped, ready for instant action. The oarsman grabs one gunwale well forward and his buddy grabs the opposite corner of the stern. Together they heave the boat forward until the hull is waterborne. Immediately the oarsman jumps in and starts rowing hard offshore.

The stern or motor-man continues to push off, waiting for exactly the proper moment to jump in. This comes when the bow is lifted by an incoming wave and the wave crest is not quite back to the stern. At this moment the stern man hops in, drops the motor, and prepares to start the motor while the oarsman continues to pull toward deep water with the oars. Once the motor is started and pushing the boat, the oars are hauled in and secured.

Returning to the beach can be exciting if there is a bit of a swell running. Here it is up to the motor-man to keep the boat surfing swiftly forward on the face of a moderate swell, going just fast enough to keep ahead of the swell's crest. At the last minute the swell will deposit the boat practically high and dry on the beach and the men can leap out quickly to haul the boat further up.

Once in a while a small open fishing boat may capsize or a fisherman may slip and fall overboard. As Charles R. Meyer once said, "Knowing how to swim helps a lot."

He and Gunnard Burgman of the Long Island Beach Buggy Association set up the series of pictures in which Gunnard deliberately fell overboard, floated in his fishing clothing supported by trapped air, then shucked his outer garments to be free to swim. Incidentally, Red Cross lifesaving classes teach swimmers how to remove their clothing in the water and how to improvise buoyant body-supports from pants or a windbreaker.

Before you try beach-launching your

(1)

(2)

Here's how to launch and return a boat with safety through a light surf:

1. Two men skid the boat to the water, the oarsman is in the forward position.

2. Boat is afloat; oarsman rows while the motorman continues to push off.

3. Oarsman continues to row while the motorman leaps into the boat.

4. Motorman starts motor, takes over propulsion of boat from oarsman.

5. Returning, boat rides the front slope of a wave until it hits the beach.

(3)

(4)

(5)

What would happen if you fell over-board? Gunard Bergman simulates such a fall.

Bergman floats, supported by a flotation jacket and air trapped in his clothing.

small boat for the first time in a running surf, go out with an experienced surf man and get the hang of it. Then, before you do it with your own boat, make sure you have taken these important precautions:

• Stow tackle boxes, lunch boxes, etc, securely under thwarts where they won't be underfoot in rough water.

• Make sure your engine is easy-starting.

• Make sure the engine is ready to start. Don't go out and forget to open the fuel tank vent.

• Time your entry into the surf to take advantage of wave wash to lift the boat's loaded hull.

• Once you decide the waves are right for the launch, don't waste any time fooling around. Get the boat water-borne and moving seaward as quickly as you can, using first the oars, then the motor when the water is deep enough.

• Don't let the boat get broadside to a cresting swell.

• Watch the sea conditions while you are out fishing. If the swell increases noticeably, head back for the beach before it becomes dangerously high.

• If you get caught outside of a danger-ous breaking surf, don't be too proud to accept a tow from a passing charter or private fishing boat that is headed for a safe harbor. That means you get in the other boat and tow your boat at the end of a rope if the water's too rough for you to make the run safely under your own power.

• Always have a good anchor handy and ready to use.

• A walkie-talkie radio is wonderful for communication with folks ashore.

• Carry an emergency flare projector in your tackle box.

• Each man should wear a flotation-type jacket or windbreaker as a matter of course.

• Carry a reserve supply of fuel. Many boats get into bad trouble when they run low on fuel and feel that they have to hit the beach in a bad surf to save them-selves.

• Let people ashore know your plan of operations and ask them to start checking things out if you don't report back to them by a specific cut-off time.

• Always be alert to the condition of other boats around you and ready to render assistance if it's needed.

Sliding like a ghost through afternoon fog, Ralph Pitts' Margaret IV *trolls for stripers on The Elbow off Montauk Light.*

6 / The Strategy of Striper Trolling

TROLLING HAS BEEN CALLED THE LAZY MAN'S way of fishing, usually by people who really should know better. Successful trollers agree that where striped bass are concerned, this fishing method requires patience, attention to details, and broad understanding of how fish react to boats and lures moving through the water. Before getting down to details, let us take a look at this "broad understanding" business. Trolling very often is the only practical way to fish for stripers, for example:

• When you have to locate fish that you know or suspect are present in an area, but can't spot from the surface of the water or from shore.

• When the stripers won't respond to casting or bait fishing.

• When your companions are inexperienced at the fishing techniques that require a considerable amount of personal fishing skill.

• When the presence of other boats makes trolling the only possible fishing method.

Most fishermen agree that stripers have varied reactions to lures trolled or retrieved in the water. What many of these fishermen fail to realize is that the fish are equally alert to and influenced by the boat itself. Fish are aware of the boat's presence through the sound field produced by the boat's propulsive equipment and its passage through the water. Fish do not "know" that the boat is not a natural creature. They accept it as part of the ocean of sound in which they live.

Very often the sound that a trolling boat makes in the water can stimulate stripers into striking at trolled lures. I saw this demonstrated some years ago at Montauk, N.Y. George Knoblach Jr., the professional skin diver and underwater photographer, was vacationing at Montauk and told me that he had discovered a large school of big bass in residence in the deep slough inside the outer bar along the ocean beach just east of Gurney's Inn. He said he'd told surf casters about the fish, but they could get no strikes and gave them up as impossible to catch.

Acting on a hunch one slow afternoon, I took my boat and charter fishing party down the beach to the place George had described. There, by golly, was Knoblach out on the water, drifting on a rubber raft, his head underwater, breathing through a snorkel tube. He told us that he was "listening to the fish," and described the characteristic thump-thump sound that fish made whenever he disturbed them by splashing from the raft.

The water was discolored by fine sand washed down from the beach by the undertow. George paddled ashore and sat down to watch while we got our tackle ready. I prescribed long yellow "Jigit" eels with pork ring strips, fished on wire line. We put the lines out and started a trolling pass westward toward Gurney's Inn.

The first pass gave us no strikes, although I could see flashes on the sounder dial that indicated big fish. Abreast of Gurney's Inn we turned and started a new pass back to the east. Just as we reached the spot where George was sitting on the

beach we got a double strike. One fish dropped the lure after a short run, but we gaffed the other, a prime 35-pounder. Five or six more passes yielded three more stripers before the fish shut the door.

For several afternoons after that I managed to sneak away from the fleet long enough to run down to the beach near Gurney's and catch a few stripers. Surf casters saw us fishing there and stopped to try their luck without success. Seldom did we get a hit on the first trolling pass. Action usually came after the second, third, or fourth pass, although I could see flashes constantly on the electronic sounder.

We could not observe the fish because of the sandy water and could only deduce what was going on. Apparently, these resident fish did not feed much during daylight hours and paid no attention to the tiny fuss made by surf casters' lures in the water. But the arrival of a boat moving at trolling speed seemed to arouse them and stimulate a few of their number into a striking mood.

Once the susceptible stripers had been caught up or stung into caution by missed strikes, the entire body of fish appeared to get tired of the boat constantly passing overhead and probably swam over the bar to deeper water outside. In any event we could not relocate them with the sounder or by blind exploratory trolling.

Another time, in clear water, I was able to observe how stripers in relatively shallow water react to a boat, and how the length of the trolling lines can be very critical in getting strikes under clear-water conditions. A friend had arrived with a new bass boat that was equipped with a small tower and asked me to guide him and his family for an afternoon.

A rod holder mounted at an angle in the corner of the cockpit holds the trolling rod out at an angle, helping to maintain a good spread to the trolling lines.

From the tower I could see the stripers closing ranks 60 feet behind the boat.

The weather had been flat calm without surf or groundswell for nearly ten days, a condition that produces very clear, uncolored water inshore. This, in turn, puts the stripers very much off their feed and on guard. We rigged up the old faithful long yellow "Jigit" eels on wire line and went down off Cottage Point for a try. There was a huge school of bass living there. You could look down from the tower and see the fish opening their ranks so the boat could pass through, then closing their ranks again back under the wake. But they wouldn't strike. Our lures, trolled at the normal line length of about 120 feet, seemed to pass right through the fish without triggering any response.

I was about to suggest that we go mackerel jigging to put some fish-smell in the box when a look into the wake from the tower with Polaroid glasses showed me that the stripers were closing ranks behind the boat at a distance of not over 60 feet from the stern. Acting again on a hunch, I asked the anglers to shorten their lines to 60 feet. No sooner had this been accomplished when a heavy double strike almost tore the rods from the hands of my friend's wife and daughter.

We gaffed the fish and resumed trolling with the lines carefully adjusted by sight from the tower to put the lures at the exact distance behind the boat where the bass were closing ranks after opening up to let the boat through. In the next hour we took eight more stripers while other boats, attracted by our activity but using lines of normal length, caught nothing.

Since then I have used this critical line length gambit successfully many times when stripers have refused to strike at what we considered to be normal line lengths for the particular spot. When water is cloudy and the fish cannot be observed, I experiment with line length by starting with a length that is only one-third of normal, and increasing the length of all lines at the same time until the correct line length for the particular situation is found.

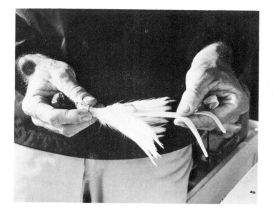

A strip of pork rind, fresh squid, or even thin, soft rubber makes many trolling lures more attractive to stripers. Besides providing body and fluttering action, the flexible strip probably also creates small, low-frequency sounds in the water similar to those made by a bait fish as it swims.

Why use lines of all the same length rather than experiment with lines of different lengths? For three very good reasons. The first is the little-known, but very potent, "school effect" that a compact formation of lures has upon the fish. If three or four lures approach a school of stripers together, they often stimulate the fish into concerted action and two, three, or even four strikes are had at the same time. This materially adds to the boat's score at the end of the day.

But if the lines are of different lengths, only one lure at a time reaches the fish and single strikes are the rule.

The second reason is that even identical-looking lures do not all fish equally well. If you are trolling three nylon eels and two keep getting strikes while the third does nothing, you quickly change that third lure. But if your lures are not together in the water so the fish can exercise choice in grabbing them, you never know which of the lures are especially hot and which may be duds.

The third reason is that lines of the same length tend to lay parallel when the boat makes turns, thereby reducing the chances of crossed lines and tangles just when the fishing starts to get hot. Furthermore, if all of the boats in a group use lines of fairly standard length, it is a lot easier for the various skippers to judge when they may turn behind other boats without fear of cutting off their lines.

Like good automobile drivers, good trollers plan their moves well in advance and operate their boats in a manner that is predictable to other skippers. They also observe special maneuvering rules whenever trolling in close company.

• They avoid excessively long lines and try to fish with lines of standard length and lure depth, using uniform boat speed, for the reasons just given.

• A boat with fish hooked is considered to have claim to the right-of-way over a boat that is trolling free.

• Boats working a small patch of fish form a circle so each will have equal chances at the fish.

• A boat never turns in front of another boat so as to force the second boat to stop or run over its lines, nor does it turn so short behind the other boat as to run over its lines.

• Anyone who accidentally cuts another's lines immediately stops to apologize and offers to replace tackle from his own stock.

• Boats approach and leave a trolling area at low speed to avoid putting the fish down.

• Boats running free give trolling boats a wide berth.

• Alert skippers suit the type of trolling

to the occasion. They don't surface-troll when everyone else is trolling deep, and they don't run across or counter to the established pattern of trolling traffic.

Putting these observations into action, let us see how experienced trollers fish several different types of situations. The first example can be a rocky headland reef extending offshore from a fairly regular shoreline, along which a tidal current tends to flow. Such a spot is King's Point a mile or so west of Montauk Light.

The small promontory that forms King's Point has a shallow cove on either side. The rocky reef extending offshore is roughly triangular in shape, with the broad base of the triangle along the shore-

line and the apex at leat 200 yards off-shore. This reef is studded with large boulders, but is safe for sport-fishing boats drawing up to four feet of water provided they exercise caution along the inshore reaches.

The best tidal current is the flood, which flows from west to east parallel to the shore. A small rip makes up along the axis of the reef, extending offshore, and marking the highest portions of the reef. The best fishing is experienced running against the current over the shallow inshore portion of the reef, then turning offshore when the lures reach the rip portion of the reef, dragging the lures offshore down the spine of rocks. This is

A fisherman hands Joe Pollio the gaff as Joe carefully leads a big striper to the side of the author's Kuno II.

Trolling pattern for a rocky point. The boat swings inshore, against the current, with all lines out and ready at "A". At "B" the boat turns offshore to "C", increasing speed to a fast troll so lures will not hang up on the rocks. The boat slows to a very slow troll by the time it has crossed the 24-foot depth line, permitting lures to sink as the water deepens. Hooked fish are recovered at "D".

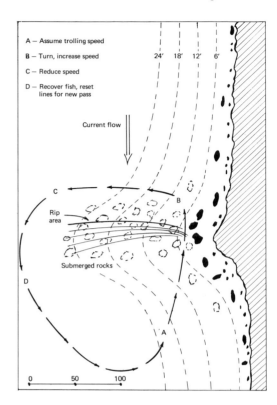

essentially a circular trolling pattern with the motion counterclockwise.

Normal trolling tackle will be Dacron, monofilament, or short wire lines with appropriate daylight, twilight, or nighttime lures. The boat approaches the point from the east, getting its lines overboard and set to the proper length, and the trolling speed regulated, while still in the cove to the east of the reef. Speed in such a case can be fairly fast, 800 to 1000 r.p.m. for standard marine engines, or four to five knots.

Conning the boat from the bridge so he can spot potentially dangerous rocks, the skipper runs roughly parallel to the shoreline, maintaining a fathom or so of depth under the boat. After passing through the rip that marks the crest of the reef extending offshore, he carefully judges distance so as to start his offshore turn just as the lures, following the boat, reach this rip. This turn is gradual, not sharp, lest lures drop too deep and foul the rocky bottom.

As the boat moves offshore, raking the reef with its lures, the skipper very carefully decreases boat speed so that as the lures find deeper water, they sink lower on the offshore pass. Some skippers may vary this routine by maintaining boat speed, but requiring the anglers to drop back line slowly as the boat moves offshore, dropping the lures as they come into deeper water.

Strikes may be had anytime during this half of the pass. If a strike is had in shallow water, the boat does not stop immediately, but continues on through the semicircular path described, the angler carefully refraining from applying too much drag pressure to the fish lest he break the line or pull out the hook. In this manner the other anglers may also get strikes before the pass has been completed. This explains the necessity for large trolling reels with what may appear, to inexperienced fishermen, to be an excessive amount of line.

At the end of the offshore pass, the boat is stopped or slowed to bare steerageway while the hooked fish are brought in for gaffing. Then the lures and lines are let out and trolling speed resumed for a fresh inshore pass. If several boats are working the same point at the same time, they form a circular pattern, out of which boats may move to fight and gaff fish, and

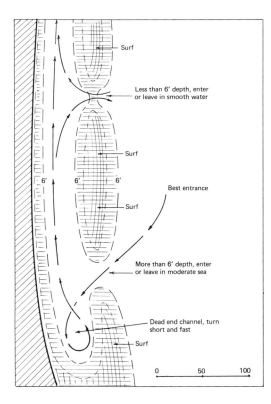

Surf

Less than 6' depth, enter or leave in smooth water

Surf

6'   6'   6'

Best entrance

Surf

More than 6' depth, enter or leave in moderate sea

Dead end channel, turn short and fast

Surf

0   50   100

Trolling pattern for an ocean bar. The boat enters the slough between bar and beach by passing through one of the deeper holes in the bar. Water inside the bar may be 15 to 20 feet deep, permitting the use of wire line tackle. Seas breaking on the bar usually spend their force before they become dangerous to the boat. Speed may be fast or slow, depending on the type of trolling lures selected.

breaks. The skipper is wise to know exactly where these breaks or deep spots are in the bar, so he can exit from the slough whenever he has to without running the danger of passing over the bar itself and possibly grounding the boat or taking a big sea over the bow.

Trolling may be done either with or against the littoral current. This is the tidal or normal current along the beach. It may or may not be related to the rise and fall of the tide in the area. Types of lures and line will depend on the situation. Generally, surface lines and lures can be used in relatively clear water, but when the water is murky with beach sand and silt, wire line and deep-trolling lures work best. Wire lines should be short enough to keep the lures from fouling bottom. At normal trolling speed, the length-depth ratio of soft-drawn, solid Monel wire is about eight-to-one. Eighty feet of wire at normal speed would put the lures down ten feet below the surface.

Trolling behind a beach bar can be tricky work if there is a sea running. Some bars, at certain levels of tide, act as sunken seawalls to break up the onshore seas, permitting boats to troll in the trough between bar and beach in relative comfort. But you always have to keep an eye seaward for the occasional big swell that may sweep completely across the bar, slough, and all.

Never enter an ocean beach bar slough when there is a sea running unless you

into which they return in due time to continue trolling.

An entirely different trolling situation is the beach trolling mentioned earlier, in which the boat works a long, narrow slough or trench between an ocean beach and the outer bar. Such bars build up along many miles of our sandy beaches, and the slough or trench between beach and bar may be from 60 to 150 yards wide and up to 15 or 20 feet deep. The bar at Gurney's Inn at the time described in the opening of this chapter was about 90 yards out from the beach, had an average depth of five feet of water over it at high tide, and protected a slough that averaged from ten to 14 feet in depth.

The best way to become familiar with a bar trench is to scout the territory thoroughly in a period of clear, calm water. All bars have occasional breaks or openings in them and the most logical entry into the slough is through one of these

know you can make the entire run from deep break to deep break safely. Some sloughs are so narrow you cannot turn without bringing in the trolling lines and then setting them out again after the turn is made. Use your sounder constantly, because some deep sloughs have a habit of slowly becoming shallower and shallower until, at the far end, the slough peters out to no water at all. This is a dead end slough and is dangerous except in fine weather.

The rules of ocean bar trolling are relatively simple. Never force another boat into a dangerous position. Be constantly on the lookout for occasional big swells, hidden rocks, and half-submerged driftwood. Always have an anchor rigged and ready. Don't tailgate the boat ahead. Stay out of trouble by never going inside a bar until you have figured out how to get back into the deep water again safely if the surf gets dangerously rough in there, or if you start to run out of water under the keel.

A much more commonly met trolling situation is that in which boats troll in, or in front of, a rip caused when a strong tidal current flows over a reef or bar in open water. Typical trolling reefs are Sow and Pigs off Cuttyhunk, Shagwong off Montauk, and Sandy Point Rip at the north end of Block Island.

A tidal current is a river in slow motion. In a river you can observe where the current flows swiftly and smoothly over a bar or submerged rock, then breaks up into rough waves on the downstream side of the obstruction. These waves, which in the salt water situation constitute the rip, are stationary with respect to the obstruction on the bottom. The shallower the water over the bar or ledge that causes the rip, the faster the tidal current is at that spot and the more violent the wave rip action will be.

By cruising over rips during the run of a tide with your electronic sounder going,

you may discover that a difference in water depth of only ten percent may be enough to form a very definite rip. Because a current of water has to speed up in order to pass over a shallower spot, the increase in velocity is in direct proportion to the decrease in depth. Thus, if you have a two-knot current in water consistently 20 feet deep, the current will measure four knots where it flows over a bar or ledge with a depth of only ten feet.

Stripers and other game fish love rip areas because of the easy feeding. Schools of small bait fish are caught in the boiling, churning currents downstream of the rip bar, and their school formations are broken up by the currents. The urge to feed when the tide is running seems built into the genes of the bass, and this very often makes it possible to predict with considerable accuracy when fishing will start and when it should stop at particular productive rip areas.

One of the nice things about a good rip is that as long as the tide runs you have a distinct observable feature that will help you stay with the fish, even in fog or darkness. Between tides, though, you may lose the bar that causes the rip unless you are able to stay with it by observing shore ranges and taking soundings with the electronic sounder.

The best practice on approaching a fishable rip is to get up-tide of the rip before slowing to trolling speed. Judge the current speed carefully because it will have a direct bearing on how you fish. For example, if the tide is horsing over the rip bar at four or five miles per hour, it would be silly to rig up with lures that troll best at two miles per hour.

Once the tackle is rigged and you have the lines out to the proper trolling distance, turn the boat down-tide toward the rip. As you come closer to the rip, make up your mind whether to turn left or right along the face of the rip. The turn should be gradual rather than sharp, and the

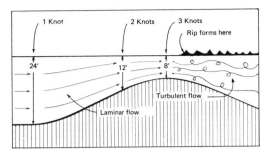

Current speed increases in proportion to the shoaling of water over a bar or ledge. A tide rip forms down-tide of the shallowest part of the bar. Striped bass inhabit a rip because turbulent current flow breaks up schools of bait, making them more vulnerable to predation.

boat should make a complete "U" turn in front of the rip, just grazing the face of the rip as it turns uptide again to maintain position before the rip.

Always remember that no matter how you turn to get into breaking fish, under feeding gulls, or to avoid other boats, your turn must be completed up-tide otherwise you will lose position in the current and have to steam hard back up-tide to get to the good fishing location.

The best fishing location in any rip is learned by fishing that rip under a wide variety of wind, tide, and weather conditions. Sometimes the fish may appear ahead of the rip in the quiet water well up-tide. Sometimes you will get your hits along the face of the rip. At other times the fish may be far back in the rough water behind the rip face.

Keeping your sounder going while fishing a rip will give you much valuable information. It will help you to keep deep-trolled lures from hanging up on the bottom. It will also familiarize you with the bottom contours of that piece of fishing territory, information that may be vital for locating the rip and the fish at night or in foggy weather.

Rip-fishing traffic sometimes gets too heavy. Outriggers for surface trolling are a waste of time in most bass fishing areas, although short outriggers for handling downrigger weights are becoming increasingly popular. In an area where rip fishing is practiced extensively, and there is little chance of hooking bass out of the rip areas, it pays to run at cruising speed from one rip to another rather than to troll experimentally over dead bottom.

Some rips seem to lend themselves to the use of particular types of lures. For example, Shagwong Reef at Montauk in late October and November is a wonderful place to troll a rigged eel at morning or evening twilight. On the other hand, the ebb rips off North Bar and Jones' Reef, down near Montauk Light, are often full of feeding bass during midday, fish that will hit almost anything that is yellow and fished with quick rod-jigging action.

This brings us to the subject of trolling lures and how they work. Basically, all lures work because they stimulate predatory fish into a striking frame of mind. We sometimes read into fish behavior certain human qualities that fish do not actually have. For example, it is probably fairly accurate to say that fish react when stimulated because of fear, hunger, territoriality, curiosity, or a desire to get rid of an annoying object. But they cannot sit back and study us the way we can observe and study them. If they could, we'd never catch them.

Trolling lures are of three basic types: those that attract visually, those that make attractive sounds in the water, and those that combine these two attributes. Most are of the third category.

Lures may also be subdivided into those that work best when trolled slowly, at moderate speed, or rapidly; those that are primarily surface lures; those that work best when trolled down deep; those that are most successful when used with jigging rod action; those that should never be jigged; and those that combine two or more of these qualities.

The following tables give a general idea of how the major categories of striper trolling lures stack up in terms of trolling position, speed, rod action, and the kind of bait present in the water.

One point may puzzle you. It is easy enough to justify marking a bullet under "Visual Attraction" for every category of lure listed, but why does each type also get a bullet under "Sound Attraction"? The answer is both complex and simple, depending on how you look at it.

Far from being the "silent world" described by Jacques Cousteau in his book and film of that name, the ocean is in reality a fairly noisy place. Fish do not have ears the way we do. They don't need them. Most fish are able to "hear" and distinguish sound and water vibrations with many parts of their bodies. The lateral line down the sides of many species of fish, for example, is a sound- and vibration-sensing organ that enables the fish to "listen" to and understand types of sound and pressure pulses in the water that are far above and below the normal range of human hearing.

Striper fishermen are familiar with the situation in which stripers refuse to strike in clear water, but take lures readily as soon as a drift of sediment or color in the water changes the visual impression. They also know that stripers have no difficulty finding and grabbing bait fish and lures in water that is almost mud where visibility is concerned.

All trolled lures make some sort of sound, although the sound pulses may be outside our narrow range of human hearing. Very often changing the sound-producing character of a lure just a little will make all the difference in the world. For instance, adding a strip of squid or pork rind to a leadhead jig may increase its fishability many fold.

Why? We don't know specifically, but we can guess that the strip of flexible pork rind or squid has the ability to make a small fluttering sound in the water that is close to that made by certain bait fish when they swim, and to which the sensory systems of the striper are acutely tuned.

A bunker spoon clatters and clanks in air and probably clanks and clicks outrageously in the water when trolled. Does it sound like a swimming mossbunker? Most probably not. But it certainly makes enough noise in the water to alert every striper within a half-mile and, when it comes gyrating by, some striper may be provoked enough to give it a smash. But there's a catch to even this theory. Bunker

Trolling Lure Depth/Action Guide

	On surface	Mid-depth	Deep-trolling	Slow speed	Medium speed	Fast speed	Visual attraction	Sound attraction	Rod action	Pork rind
Natural eels		•	•	•	•		•	•		
Plastic eels		•	•	•	•		•	•		
Eelskins		•	•	•	•		•	•		
Nylon eels	•	•			•	•	•	•	•	•
Leadhead jigs	•	•	•		•	•	•	•	•	•
Small spoons	•	•	•	•	•		•	•		•
Bunker spoons		•	•	•	•		•	•		
Tube lures		•	•	•	•		•	•		
Trolling plugs	•	•	•	•	•	•	•	•		
Plastic fish		•	•				•	•		
Streamer flies	•	•		•	•		•	•	•	
Metal jigs	•	•	•		•	•	•	•	•	•

Observe This Bait? Then Use This Tackle

Bait observed	Lures for trolling	How fished
Bunkers Herring Alewives	Bunker spoons, big swimming plugs, large feathers with squid strips or porkrind	Troll deep, little or no rod action
Whiting Red hake Porgies	Large swimming plugs, big feathers and strips, nylon eels and strips, spoons	Surface or deep, slow rod action
Mullet Snappers Sardines	Feather or nylon skirt jigs and porkrind, nylon eels, bucktails, parrot-bills	Surface or deep, quick rod action
Sand eels Spearing Silversides	Small bucktails, nylon jigs, spoons, feather lures with squid or porkrind strips	Surface or deep, quick rod action
Squid Anchovies	White-and-yellow jigs with strips, nylon eels, spoons, long thin swimming plugs	Surface or deep, easy rod action
Mackerel Weakfish	Mackerel-finish diving plugs, yellow-and-green feathers and nylon eels, squid or porkrind	Deep and slow, little or no rod action
Baby scup Blowfish Flatfish	Orange-yellow-white feather and nylon jigs and eels, pork strips, short tubing eels	Surface or deep, easy rod action
Black eels	Rigged natural or plastic eels, eelskins, long tube lures, black-and-white nylon eels	Deep and slow without rod action
Sand or blood worms	Spinner-and-worm rigs, long thin tube lures, shoestring eelskins, trolling flies	Deep and slow drifting or 1–2 m.p.h.

spoons don't seem to work well unless bunkers are present and the stripers have become accustomed to feeding on them.

So even the most painstakingly contrived explanations have to be taken with a shakerful of salt. The smart striper fisherman reserves judgement and belief in theories until successful catching proves them worth believing.

This business of learning how and what to observe, and how to interpret the things you see, is vital to successful striper trolling. For example, everyone is familiar with the old exhortation to "follow the birds" to fishing action, but when you get to where the birds are feeding on surface bait and other boats are hauling in stripers right and left—and you catch nothing —the situation becomes quite binding.

If you are trolling in the same water

with other boats that are catching stripers while you are not, the first thing you must do is to *use psychology on yourself* so your powers of observation and analysis will not be blinded by your disgust and frustration. Then follow a definite pattern of checks to find out what you are doing wrong.

One of the first things to check is the kind of lure that the successful boats are using. Same as yours? Fine. The trouble is something else. Different lure? Switch to what they are using. Next, how fast are they trolling? After you have fished for a while you will recognize that certain types of lures have specific trolling speeds at which they work best. Are you going too slow for the lures that are catching the fish? Most boats commit the sin of trolling too slowly rather than too fast.

Match speed with the other boats at the exact moment when they are passing over the good fishing spots. Remember that most skippers tend to slow down after hooking fish and, conversely, tend to speed up beyond maximum effective trolling speed while coming around

through "dead water" for another trolling pass over good bottom.

With lures and speed carefully matched to the successful boats, are you still drawing a blank? Probably your line length is wrong, especially if you are using wire line for deep trolling. The depth ratio of lures trolled with wire line is a direct function of speed. Suppose you find the boats are all trolling slightly faster than usual for that spot and those lures. What does this suggest?

It immediately suggests that, to get the lures down to the effective depth, they are fishing wire lines longer than usual. How can you find out without asking them? It's not hard if you know what to look for.

The majority of the boats may be in the habit of spooling, say, 150 feet of wire on each reel. At this spot they normally troll with just a few turns of wire left on the reel spool. Do you now see them trolling with all the wire out and perhaps 40 or 50 feet of soft-line backing back from the rod tips? If so, this is sure evidence that they are trolling just a wee bit faster than usual and putting out at least 60 feet of

extra line to achieve the optimum lure depth.

Try this with all lines adjusted to the same length and with the speed increased by, say, one mile per hour, and you may almost immediately start to get strikes.

What to do if the other boats are using so much wire on their reels it is impossible to determine line length for the amount of backing line exposed? This is really not so difficult. For example, you should know exactly how many turns of the average reel handle it takes to reel in 100 feet of wire or other line. On the average 3/0 or 4/0 reel, it takes around 70 reel handle turns to bring in the first 100 feet, a few less turns for each succeeding 100 feet.

Knowing this, wait until you see an angler or mate on a successful boat reel in a fishing line to inspect the lure or change the pork rind. Mentally count how many turns of the reel handle it takes to bring in the lure. If it takes 200 turns this is a good indication then that he is fishing with at least 300 feet of wire line out. If you are fishing 200 feet or 250, put out enough extra line to match his line length and increase your trolling speed to the point where you are in no danger of hanging the lures on the bottom.

Finally, if you were to ask me what single precaution is most important to successful striper trolling, I would have to tell you about something that is so simple many fishermen don't give it a first thought, let alone serious second consideration. This is that to get hits on trolled lures, your lures must be *scrupulously clean.*

By clean I don't mean laundered with soap and water after each use. I mean picked clean of the small bits of sea weed, shoestring grass, straw, sponge, sticks, and other debris that fish hooks constantly pick up when they are trolled on lures through the water. The only way to be sure the hooks are clean is to set up a system for hauling in each line at frequent intervals whenever the water is dirty, as it frequently is after a storm or during a period of perigee tides.

When deep trolling you should make it an established rule always to haul in a line when the lure is suspected of touching the bottom. Just a tiny bit of weed, grass, or filament of algae is enough to destroy the attractiveness of the lure's appearance, sound, and action in the eyes of the stripers. Your purpose in trolling is to catch fish, not to tow trouble behind the boat all day.

Trolling may indeed be the ideal fishing method for some lazy fishermen, but the real striper angler recognizes it as a system that produces when other methods fail, provided the fisherman is not lazy and uses the proper strategy.

Wire line tackle is sure-fire for getting trolling lines down deep. Harry Clemenz, Sr., gaffs up a husky Montauk striper taken on deep trolling tackle.

FRANK T. MOSS

7 / The Science of Deep Trolling

DEEP TROLLING FOR GAME FISH, ESPECIALLY for striped bass, is now much more of a science than it was just a few years ago. There are four basic ways of achieving depth with trolling lures: by using wire line, by adding heavy trolling sinkers to soft fishing lines, by employing downriggers to carry soft line lures down deep, and by using lures that are self-diving through weight, shape, or a combination of both. Let us look at the four systems in the order just given.

The use of wire line for deep trolling started in the Great Lakes before World War II when pleasure and commercial fishermen found that soft-drawn copper wire and big sinkers would take metal spoons down 100 feet or more to catch the lake trout and other big fish that abounded in the lakes at that time.

Shortly after World War II, soft-drawn, solid Monel wire became popular among Florida commercial handlining kingfishermen for deep trolling. This commercial heritage has tainted the use of wire line in the eyes of some sportsmen. The International Game Fish Association, for example, does not recognize catches of fish made with wire line. But this does not stop millions of sport fishermen from using this versatile, very successful fishing tool.

Even those who profess to hate wire line with an almost religious fervor admit that it has opened vast new areas to successful deep trolling, areas that never before were suspected of containing fish that could be caught with rod and reel.

Wires popular for deep trolling include nylon-covered lead-core line, braided Monel, and solid, soft-drawn Monel. Of these, the last-mentioned is by far the most popular with striped bass anglers. Soft-drawn solid Monel is available in a variety of gauges. The following table gives the approximate breaking strain of soft Monel wire in terms of diameter, which is measured in thousandths of an inch:

Wire diameter	Approx. test
.015"	15 lb.
.018"	25 lb.
.021"	35 lb.
.024"	45 lb.
.027"	55 lb.
.030"	70 lb.

Some grades of Monel wire may test slightly higher or lower than these average figures. Solid wire line has a limited life under salt water conditions, especially when jigging rod action is used. Therefore, most striper fishermen fill their reels half to two-thirds full of quality soft line backing and splice just enough wire on top of this to do the work at hand. The backing line is usually Dacron or monofilament line with a rated test slightly heavier than that of the wire being used. For example, my own personal pair of deep trolling rods were made up in the following manner:

Rods. Matched pair of soft-action fiberglass shafts rated for line of 40 to 50 pound test. Roller guides and roller tip-top. Locking reel seat on separate boat-rod butt

59

with universal gimbal fitting at lower end.

Reels. Pair of Penn Long Beach #67 star drag reels of approximately 4/0 size. These have wide, open spools with no cross-bar across the top of the spool face. Gear ratio is a moderate 2 1/2: 1.

Backing. Spools are filled 2/3 full with quality 50 pound test Dacron trolling line, approximately 175 yards.

Wire. 100 yards of .024″ soft-drawn solid Monel wire is spliced onto the backing line. This wire tests about 45 pounds breaking strain and is terminated with a small, strong stainless steel snap swivel. Wire is marked every 100 feet with a special wrapping of waterproof friction tape and dental floss that is color-coded to indicate the amount of wire let out from the reel.

Many anglers like the Penn Senators in 3/0 and 4/0 sizes. These are excellent reels for big stripers on wire line. I happen to prefer the Long Beach model because of its lighter weight and wider, more open spool. The drag washers and main and pinion gears of the Long Beach reels are softer and wear out more easily than those of the Senator series, but these parts are cheap and easy to replace.

The methods of measuring and splicing wire line to backing are described elsewhere in this book. Beginners in using wire often have difficulty in stripping the wire out from the reel when letting out line. The correct procedure follows:

1. Set the boat's speed for a fast troll, four to five knots, and set a straight course. Determine the length of wire to be put out by consulting your depth sounder and local chart.

2. Engage the clicker of the reel, then place the thumb of the hand holding the rod and reel onto the reel spool. Finally, slack back the drag to a low value of line tension (don't throw the reel on free spool!).

3. Strip wire from the reel with the other hand, stripping against the combined tension of clicker, thumb, and moderate reel drag. Work the rod tip back and forth with "body English" to free the stripped wire through the rod guides and into the water behind the boat. Practice will show you how to do this quickly and efficiently.

4. When you have stripped out 60 to 70 feet, check to see if the weight of wire now in the water is enough to drag more wire from the reel without further manual stripping.

5. When the proper length of wire is out, reset the reel drag to the proper tension and disengage the clicker before placing the rod in a rod holder or starting to jig it by hand to apply rod action to the lure. Because wire has absolutely no stretch at all, you lose the spring effect that soft line gives you between rod and lure. Therefore, the reel drag should be set to easy tension. The following table gives a useful rule of thumb for setting drag tension with different grades of solid wire.

Approx. test	Reel drag
15 lb.	3 lb.
25 lb.	5 lb.
35 lb.	7 lb.
45 lb.	9 lb.
55 lb.	11 lb.
70 lb.	14 lb.

Observing two rules will help you to avoid getting backlashes on your reel as you put out the wire.

1. *Never* start stripping wire out until you have engaged the reel's clicker and placed a thumb on the spool to prevent the spool from overrunning or back-spinning.

2. *Always* reel in wire line slowly and with care, using the thumb of the rod-holding hand to lay the wire evenly back and forth across the spool. Never let wire pile up in parallel turns at any spot on the spool. This will ensure smooth, easy, let-

ting-out of the wire when you start to strip back the next time.

As a rule of thumb, solid Monel wire of .021″ to .024″ diameter, the most popular sizes, will carry a one-ounce leadhead jig or lure, trolled at the standard speed of three to four knots, down one foot for every eight feet of wire in the water. This 8:1 ratio means that 100 feet of wire, in the water, will put the one-ounce lure down to a depth of 12 1/2 feet at normal trolling speed.

Using normal trolling speed and the one-ounce lure as a base, the following table gives trolling depths achieved by various lengths of wire:

Water depth	Best lure depth	Wire length
10′	8′	64′
20′	17′	136′
30′	26′	208′
40′	35′	280′
50′	44′	352′

Because of its complete lack of stretch, solid wire line is ideal for applying jigging rod action to jigging lures. The best position for jigging is standing up with the rod tip held in an inverted position, the tip just brushing the surface of the water. The most commonly used jigging tempo is a short, quick rod-chop applied at the rate of 120 chops per minute, or the same tempo as a military march step.

If you think "left, right, left, right . . ." in march tempo as you jig, the tempo will be correct for small jig-type lures. Don't make long, sweeping moves of the rod. The rod tip should move only about a foot at most, and quickly enough so the wire line just snaps taut against the rod tip at the end of each stroke.

This action, transfered down the long, inelastic wire, will set the lure to dancing and waltzing in the water in a manner that stripers find almost irresistable. Jigging can be a fine art and those who know

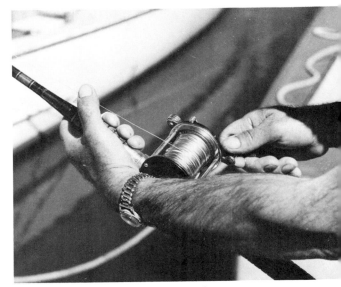

Wire line should be laid on evenly across the spool of a wide-framed reel.

how to vary the rhythm according to the lures in use and the fishing conditions vastly increase their chances of success at the science of deep trolling.

After the proper lengths of wire have been paid out for the depth of water and the reel drags adjusted to the proper value for the gauge of wire being used, you can place the rods in rod holders arranged to give a good spread to the lines (if you are using non-jigging lures), or you can instruct the anglers to start the proper jigging technique. Having all of the wires out to exactly the same length is doubly advantageous.

The lines lay parallel in the water when the boat makes turns, thus avoiding line tangles. The lures swim through the water in fairly close proximity to each other, providing the desirable "school effect" discussed elsewhere in this book.

The ability to control lure depth is important, and there are several ways to achieve this. Length of wire paid out is one. Increasing or lowering trolling speed is another. Raising the speed from three to four or five knots will raise the level of the lures by about one-quarter or one-third, respectively, of the depth held at three knots.

Thus, if you are trolling in 20 feet of water with 135 feet of wire out, holding a lure depth of about 17 feet, and suddenly spot a 15-foot bar taking shape under the boat (using your electronic sounder), you can raise the lures to a safe 12-foot level by boosting the speed to five knots for the time it takes to drag them over the shallower bar.

Changing to heavier lures will increase the trolling depth, with the same length of wire, by a factor of about 10 feet of depth per ounce of lure head weight, provided boat speed stays the same. The same effect can be obtained by inserting a small trolling sinker between the end of the wire line and the upper end of the lure leader. Here, leaders should be monofilament or light wire at least 50 percent heavier than the main wire, and at least 12 feet long.

Even light trolling sinkers have a tendency to dampen the effectiveness of rod jigging action, but they often help to solve the problem of heavy boat traffic and long lines when the fish will respond to non-jigging lures. For example, if the water is 40 feet deep and you have been trolling bare wires about 280-feet long to put the lures at the desired 35-foot depth, you can achieve the same depth with the same weight of lure by inserting a four-ounce trolling sinker between wire and leader and reducing the line length to approximately 150 feet. You may also have to change the type of lure to get hits.

One bugaboo of fishing with wire line is how to deal with the kinks that inevitably form in the wire from careless handling. The best way, of course, is to keep them from forming by always maintaining a light strain on the wire, and by carefully leveling the wire onto the reel spool as you wind it in.

If a kink starts to form, but is still open and not drawn up tightly, you can usually open the kink by unbending the wire against the direction in which the kink was made. But if the kink has been drawn tight and the wire is distorted at that spot, the only recourse is to cut out the kink with your wire pliers and splice the wire. Properly made, the resulting splice is flexible, will render through the rod guides and store easily on the reel spool, and is at least 80 percent as strong as the original wire.

Another trouble peculiar to wire line is that wire tends to become brittle with prolonged use and may fail under very light or no apparent strain because of crystallization of the fatigued metal. Jigging, especially, seems to fatigue soft-drawn Monel wire. When wire becomes hard-feeling under the fingers in stripping out, this is a sure sign that fatigue has set in. The best cure is to replace the entire fatigued wire with fresh material.

As your experience with wire grows, you'll learn tricks that the pros use to cut corners. Charter boat mates, for instance, often engage the clicker and slack off the drag of the wire line reel, then place the rod in a handy side rod holder while they strip out the line from the rod tip with a smooth, constant, hand-over-hand hauling motion.

They also will put out a wire while the boat is making a change of course. The secret of putting out wire while the boat is making a turn is always to strip out the wire from the boat's side that is on the outside of the turn. For example, if the boat is turning to port, strip the wire out from the starboard side and you'll avoid tangling with the wires that are already fishing. If you try to strip out a wire from the boat's side that is on the inside of the turn, your wire will drift back into and tangle with the lines that are fishing.

A wise skipper never makes a turn of more than 90 degrees when trolling with wire, lest the lures sink and snag bottom. The longer the wires, the deeper and slower they will tow when the boat makes turns. If you have to turn quickly to avoid other boats, speed up or have the fishermen reel in their wires at least halfway.

IGFA tackle rules specifically forbid using wire line, so record-seekers and anglers who dislike using wire have to find some other means of getting their lures down deep when fish they seek refuse to strike on or near the surface. One of the oldest "legal" methods of doing this is to add a trolling sinker to the soft line between the end of the line and the forward end of the leader.

Trolling sinkers are cigar-shaped pieces of lead weighing from 1/4-ounce to as much as two pounds, equipped with a brass or stainless steel connecting eye at each end. The snap swivel at the end of the fishing line is fastened to one eye and the lure leader to the other. The leader in this case is usually at least six feet long and may be as much as 12 or 15 feet from sinker to lure. It can be monofilament or light stainless steel wire.

Let's compare a 100-foot length of standard wire line with an equal length of Dacron or mono of the same strength. It will take a sinker of six ounces weight to carry a one-ounce lead-head lure to the 12 1/2-foot depth that the wire can achieve at the standard trolling speed of about four knots. Exceptionally light soft lines, of course, will require less sinker weight. The parasitic drag of the sinker and soft line will be approximately four times as great as that of the wire.

Because of the lift-effect of the line moving through the water and the greater surface friction of soft lines, doubling the

A keel sinker will prevent line from twisting when using lures that spin.

length of line or the applied weight will achieve only about an 80 percent increase in depth. If the line length is kept constant, the increasing angle of attack as weight is added to gain depth also has an inhibiting effect on the depth achieved.

The table below puts together the sinker weights needed to achieve given depths when a standard one-ounce lure is trolled on 100 feet of 50-pound-test mono or high-grade Dacron line at the fairly normal speed of four knots.

Remember that these figures are approximations and that you may achieve results somewhat different from these. Monofilament line of some types, for example, may differ from certain Dacron lines of the same line test by as much as 10 percent greater depth for the same weight, speed, and line length.

The table shows that as depth increases, the amount of weight you must add to achieve the desired depth increases at a considerably more rapid rate. There is a very definite limit to the amount of sinker weight you can fish on rod and reel while trolling with comfort

Water depth	Lure depth	Sinker weight	Line length	Speed
10'	8'	4 oz.	100'	4 kn.
15'	12 1/2'	7 oz.	100'	4 kn.
20'	16'	11 oz.	100'	4 kn.
25'	20'	16 oz.	100'	4 kn.
30'	25'	22 oz.	100'	4 kn.

The downrigger is an underwater outrigger. The "bomb" carries the fishing line and lure to the desired depth. When a fish strikes, the line is pulled from the release clip, and the angler reels in the fish unencumbered.

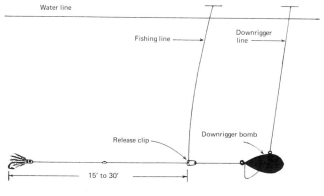

and effectiveness. For most people, using lures designed for medium speed, six to eight ounces of sinker weight is quite enough, and 100 feet of line is plenty. This limits trolling sinkers to waters of 15 to 18 feet in depth for medium-speed and high-speed lures, and certainly to not much more than 25 feet in depth for even the slowest-moving lures.

One way to use trolling sinkers in very deep water is to troll very slowly with medium-speed or high-speed lures and supply the extra needed lure speed by constantly heaving and hauling with rod and reel. The heave-and-haul method works this way:

The boat is set on a straight course, barely stemming the current, and the lures are dropped all the way to the bottom. Thumb the spool of the reel strongly to prevent the leader and the fishing line from twisting together as the trolling sinker drags the lure down deep. Sinkers of six to eight ounces weight are normally used regardless of water depth.

As soon as the sinker touches bottom, it is lifted off the bottom by a quick lift of the rod tip and the angler begins reeling in the line at a retrieve speed of one or two turns of the reel handle per second. Strikes are had within a few feet of the bottom in most cases. If no strike has been obtained by the time the lure has been raised 20 feet from the bottom, the lure is dropped back again and the hauling-in process repeated.

Three drops to the bottom are usually about as many as the angler can make before reeling the lure all the way back to the surface to regain expended line. Practiced properly, this can be very productive on bluefish, cod, pollock, and school stripers where these fish are schooled near the bottom in water of from 25 to over 100 feet deep.

Good lures for heaving and hauling are lead-head jigs with squid or pork rind strips, small spoons, Japanese feathers

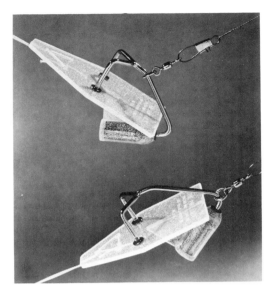

The Pink Lady is a planer that achieves depth by being towed at the proper angle of attack (upper planer). When a fish strikes, the pull trips the planer out of the diving position (lower), making it easier to retrieve for further use.

with squid strips, eelskins, and tube lures. An interesting variation of this technique is to substitute big diamond jigs weighing from six to ten ounces for the combination of trolling sinker and lure. Diamond jigs can be fished with the heave-and-haul routine, or jigged directly off the bottom in the more classic manner.

Back in the late 1930s, when I was learning the fishing business as a mate on Montauk charter boats, we had a deep trolling system that combined heaving and hauling with rod and reel with the use of underwater outriggers. It worked this way: Two or three rods with eight-ounce trolling sinkers and Japanese feathers tipped with squid were worked in the heave-and-haul method off the boat's stern while two more lines were trolled deep by means of underwater outriggers hung from short pipes extending out from the boat's sides. The latter two lines employed big feathers, spoons, or eelskin lures that did not depend on any kind of rod action for attracting the stripers.

The underwater outriggers were ten-pound sash weights or gooseneck drails on the ends of stout, tarred Sea Island cotton handlines. The handlines were rove through small pulleys at the end of the short pipe outriggers. First I would stream a side line 15 or 20 feet behind the boat. Then I would clip the fishing line into a snap-jaw clothespin attached to the trailing end of the heavy weight. Finally I would lower the weight to the end of its line while the angler at the same time let out fishing line.

When a strike was had on the downrigger, the fish yanked the line clear of the clothes pin and I would haul the weight to the surface again and clip in another angler's line and lure, often before the first fisherman had brought his fish up to gaff. Between heaving and hauling at the stern and downrigging from the sides, we often had what amounted to a conveyor belt of fish coming in over the stern.

In recent years ultra-modern versions of the downrigger have found great favor among Great Lakes salmon fishermen and are starting to be used on both the East and West Coasts by deep trolling striper anglers. Modern downriggers use heavy-gauge solid Monel wire to carry the cannonball weights. The wire reels are so constructed that each turn of the reel handle takes in or lets out exactly two feet of support wire.

Downriggers are especially useful

where the water is quite deep, or where there is a very strong tidal current. You can construct your own downriggers by spooling heavy tuna line onto old 6/0 offshore reels until the reels are nearly full. Try to arrive at a reel diameter of backing line that will enable you to take in two feet or three feet of, say, .030″ solid Monel carrying line with each turn of the reel handle. Mark this wire at appropriate depths.

Mount the downrigger reels on old, heavy tuna rods that can be locked into rod holders holding the rods out at an angle from the boat's sides. The weights can be five-pound or heavier lead gooseneck drails or plain cast lead balls. The commercially sold "Fire Island Drop-Back" clip, or a snap-jaw clothes pin reinforced with rubber bands, will make a good line release.

In all deep trolling, no matter what the method, success depends in large part on correctly reading the water depth, the depth at which the fish are swimming, and the effect of currents and wind on the depth attained by the lures. A strong wind on the bow will slow a boat down, often causing lures to foul the bottom. On the stern, the same wind may increase the boat's speed to the point that the lures are many feet too high for the fish. Learning how to compensate for wind effect is a matter of experience and judgement.

The fourth and final method of deep trolling that we want to know about is the comparatively new business of using lures that attain depth by their own weight and action. Modern plug manufacturers have created many new designs of plugs that are able to dive deeply when retrieved. Many of these are adaptable to deep trolling. Diving and swimming action is usually attained by means of a long, broad metal lip in front of the plug's head, to which the towing ring or clip is attached.

If you want to experiment with self-diving plugs, there are a couple of points to remember. One is that while the IGFA (as of this writing) accepts catches made on plugs containing not more than two gang or treble hooks, the fish must be taken by casting and retrieving, not by trolling. To modify these plugs for trolling under IGFA tackle rules, you must remove the gang or treble hooks and install not more than two single hooks.

Many anglers, on hearing this, immediately complain that this alteration will destroy the action and fish-catching ability of the plug. My answer is, how do they know until they've tried it? Some of the best lures we have today resulted from modification of other lures, changes that so-called experts swore wouldn't work. They work if they catch fish, and there's only one way to find out. Give the modified plug or lure a good, honest test and if it doesn't work the first time, try some more.

Deep trolling imposes certain disciplines on fishermen. Speed must be held to exact values. The depth of water cannot be just guessed at. Turns must be made smoothly and evenly and planned well in advance. But it is a system that puts fish into the angler's box when other methods do not. One measure of a well-rounded striped bass fisherman is how well he can adapt his knowledge and equipment to take fish when other anglers fail. Deep trolling often provides the key to this problem.

8 / The Art of Bucktailing

"I'VE GOT ONE!" SCOTTY SHOUTED AS HE slammed all his 45 pounds into the arching spinning rod and waited as the striper ran off a dozen fathoms of line against the drag. The tussle ended when his father, Doug, gaffed the fat school bass and dropped it into the fish box.

It was mid-April and the water temperature of New Jersey's Great Bay and Mullica River finally had topped 50°, the magical temperature at which stripers start to take lures along the Jersey shore in the spring. For the past three weeks the stripers had been caught mostly at night on bloodworms, but now the fish were hitting bucktail jigs with a vengeance and everyone on boats around us was lifting fish over the side.

Surprisingly enough, the only lures that these fish would hit were small lead-headed, bucktail-skirted jigs in weights of 1/4 to 1/2 ounce. The fish ran from little 14-inchers up to a good ten pounds, with an occasional 20-pound lunker thrown in. It seemed impossible that the fish would strike only bucktail jigs, so we experimented with floating and sinking plugs, rubber worms, small spoons, and other lure combinations without hooking fish. As soon as we switched back to yellow or white bucktails the fish took hold with a will.

This particular morning there must have been more than 100 boats drifting with the tide and wind on Great Bay at the mouth of the Mullica River. Anytime we looked around the fleet we could see someone hooking into, fighting, or lifting out a hard-fighting little striper.

The tide was now almost slack and I flipped a bucktail up into the wind and let it sink to the bottom in about 15 feet of water. Then I gave the rod tip a quick flip to make the jig jump on the bottom, and started turning the handle of the reel slowly as I began the retrieve. The art of bucktailing, Jersey-style, is to make the bucktail jig bounce along the bottom, not too fast, but with enough action to challenge the feeding instincts of the stripers that have not yet started to feed heavily after spending the winter in a semi-dormant state in the upper reaches of the Mullica River.

The bucktail had bounced along the bottom for about 20 feet when I felt the solid smack of a good strike. In the spring, more often than not, the striper will hook himself when he picks up the bucktail. To be on the safe side I gave the rod a quick lift. The striper surfaced and tossed spray before calling it quits. It was a wee one, well under the 18-inch New Jersey minimum length. I unhooked it carefully and dropped it into the water. We were glad to see so many of these little fellows. They represented a successful spawning season two or three years before in Chesapeake Bay, and also in the upper reaches of the Mullica and other Jersey rivers.

The ebb tide went slack for an hour, so we ate sandwiches. When the flood tide began we really socked it to the stripers. Scotty hooked several fish and fought them to a standstill. The only help the boy needed was in gaffing or netting the fish.

He had mastered the spincasting rod and was dropping bucktails 60 feet out like a veteran. This was one of the days you dream about when you plan to take a boy fishing. The fish bite and he gets action. Hook a boy on fishing early in life and he'll be yours forever.

We released about a dozen bass in the under-18-inch class and boated four that weighed between three and eight pounds. We saw several ten-pounders taken on nearby boats, and one angler showed us a fish that must have weighed at least 20 pounds. He had taken it in Grassy Channel early in the morning.

Almost without exception the fish were taken on bucktails averaging about 1/4-ounce in weight, either white, yellow, or white-and-yellow in color. This little chunk of lead and deer-tail hair is probably the most consistent bass-killer for early-season fishing on the market, and it does not stop taking fish until early winter puts a stop to all striper fishing. If I were limited to just one lure for stripers, it would be a white-and-yellow bucktail jig.

Exactly why the bucktail is so deadly on stripers is hard to say. To me it doesn't resemble any object, animal, vegetable, or mineral, that a striper might encounter in its natural habitat. But it does have lively action and it may stimulate the same reaction in stripers that they would take in sight of a fleeing shrimp, crab, or bait fish. It goes straight to the bottom, requiring very little "countdown." If fished properly at the right places, close to the bottom, it strikes paydirt as the best spring striper lure.

When stripers leave the deep holes in the tidewater rivers where they have spent the winter months, they follow warm water out into the bays and finally out into the ocean. They are highly sensitive to temperature changes. A cold spell and falling temperatures will send them right back up into the rivers again.

Until late April and May, when spear-ing, shrimp, sea worms, and other natural bait come to life, these coastal stripers feed very little even though they will strike lures the way migrating salmon will strike flies. Most of the fish have empty and shrunken stomachs. They spend most of their time on the bottom and probably hit lures out of irritation, curiosity, or because of an awakening sense of hunger. The bucktail appears to be the one lure that has the weight, small size, and lively action that goads these semi-dormant fish when almost all other lures fail.

Exactly where and how it originated is hard to say. Morrie Upperman of Atlantic City and Allen Corson of Ocean City, N.J., and later of Florida, did a lot to popularize the bucktail jig. Morrie Upperman caught a New Jersey state record striper that weighed 63 pounds 10 ounces at Barnegat Inlet in 1960 on an Upperman bucktail.

Morrie, with his brother Bill, began making bucktails commercially back in 1937. Along came World War II and the Navy awarded them the contract for supplying the hundreds of thousands of 3/o bucktails that went into lifeboat and life raft survival kits carried on Navy and Merchant Marine ships, and by Naval aviators. Experimentation had proved that the bucktail was the one lure that would catch fish almost anywhere, under the most extreme conditions.

Color of bucktails seems to be highly important on certain days, and even on different tides. The most popular colors are white, yellow, white-and-yellow, white-and-red, in about that order, but many other colors sell and also catch fish. The Florida hot pinks, for example, have been quite popular recently. At one time black-and-purple was a hot combination, although I suspect it caught more fishermen than stripers.

There are days when white will outfish all other colors, and the reverse is true.

Young Scotty McLain (above) ties into a New Jersey striper taken on a jigged bucktail. He and his father (left) show part of an afternoon's catch. Bucktail jigging is highly effective in many Atlantic and Pacific striper areas.

Lead-head bucktail jigs come in a wide variety of sizes, shapes, and colors.

Sometimes white just doesn't make the grade. I recall one day when my good friend Dr. Bernie Levine was fishing with me at the mouth of the Forked River in Barnegat Bay. Bernie was taking one fish after another with a 1/4-ounce yellow bucktail and I never had a hit, fishing with an identical 1/4-ounce white jig right next to him. When he had eight fish in the boat I swallowed my pride, switched to yellow, and quickly was taking my share.

During the April trip mentioned in opening, Doug, Scotty, and I fished with mixed lures and the fish showed no measurable preference for one color over another. But success with mixed lures is the exception rather than the rule. This is why most successful bucktail artists carry a wide selection of lures and change lures often until they find the exact combination that works best for a given place, state of tide, day, and temper of the fish.

Along the Jersey coast in the spring, schools of stripers follow the river channels, using them as roadways to and from their winter up-river habitats. Success with bucktails often depends on being able to interpret how and where the fish are moving in light of recent weather changes, especially changes in water temperature. If you can locate one of these roving schools, you'll have fast and furious action.

As the waters warm, the bass move out of the deep channels and up onto the sandy flats in as little as two feet of water. This is where tidal bay fishing is at its best. The fish suddenly awaken to their hunger and gorge on sandeels, spearing, shrimp, or whatever bait is there. At times like these they will hit any lure that is presented to them in the water, provided it is consistent with the bait they are feeding on.

There are several techniques for fishing the bucktail. Wind, current, floating grass, and other conditions may require that you alter your technique to make the bucktail behave properly. Some anglers prefer to cast into the wind so the bucktail

Bucktailers carry a large assortment of jigs to satisfy fickle striper moods.

drifts behind the boat as it is retrieved. They regulate the speed of retrieve so they can just feel the bucktail touch bottom every time they flick the tip of the rod. In a strong wind or tide, a heavier bucktail must be used to hold bottom.

Anglers who prefer the lightest bucktails usually cast downwind or downtide and retrieve more rapidly to make up for the speed of the drift. Here the rule of the thumb is this:

• Casting up-tide and upwind, retrieve slowly

• Casting down-tide and downwind, retrieve faster.

Of course, it's also possible to cast across the wind or current, off the side of the boat, and this often has to be done if there are several anglers all fishing together. The important thing is to feel the jig actually bouncing on the bottom as you reel in and jig the tip of the road with short, quick lifts to impart action to the bucktail.

Where the tidal current is very fast, a good stunt is to drop the jig directly down without casting out and jig it vertically on the bottom as you might for mackerel. This is effective when there is much eel grass in the water. Ken Buntain and Dick Lyons of Forked River use the vertical jigging technique in grass-rich Barnegat Bay and probably catch more stripers during the season than any of the other local Indians.

For deep water, heavier bucktails are needed. In water less than 20 feet deep (most of the Jersey bay waters fit into this category) you can usually get by with a 1/2 to 3/4 ounce bucktail if the tide isn't too strong. A good rule is to use the smallest and lightest jig that will do the job of fishing bottom under prevailing wind and tide conditions.

Plastic detergent jugs are frequently anchored in the bays to mark the schools. When fishing is good you may see a dozen bleach jugs bobbing around you. The trouble is that other fishermen usually have no compunctions about using your

Boyd Pfeiffer tied these hand-made jigs.

marker. This is not too bad if the boats, in moving upwind and up-tide for fresh drifts, do so at moderate speed so as not to spook the fish. Unfortunately, some clown usually can't take his time. He speeds up over the school and there goes your fishing for the afternoon.

Most of the boats now fishing stripers use sounders of one kind or another. These units reveal the depth of water, give you an idea of the character of the bottom, and often reveal fish under the boat. A good sounder is a great help in locating deep-swimming schools.

When the fish are deep, finding them is often a hide-and-seek proposition, but as the weather warms and the stripers move onto the flats, their feeding activity is often marked by flocks of gulls and terns wheeling over the bait fish driven to the surface by the stripers. In foggy weather we can sometimes actually smell the feeding fish, a faint fragrant aroma somewhat like that of freshly cut melon.

A good jigging rod is a fishing tool to be cherished. You can take stripers with almost any type of spinning or bait-casting rod, but some rods work the jigs better and catch more fish than others. A good rod for bucktail jigging is in the six to seven foot tip length range with a soft tip, but with enough backbone in the lower section to allow you to put pressure on fish that may go to 20 or more pounds.

Needless to say, the rod's action should be balanced to the weight of the lures you use. It would be impractical to try to jig a heavy, four-ounce jig with a soft-tipped rod designed to work with lures in the 1/4 to 1/2 ounce range. Generally speaking, these are the most popular jig weights used in the Jersey bays. If you go offshore, or fish the deeper rivers and bay channels in strong tides, you'll need heavier jigs and a heavier rod.

Boat-launching sites are no problem in the Great Bay and Barnegat Bay areas. There are tackle shops and boat ramps on Great Bay Boulevard east of Tuckerton, at the Great Bay Marina at Gravelling Point, at Stan Cramer's Chestnut Neck Boat Yard just a stone's throw from the Garden State Parkway, and at Mott Creek and Oyster Creek along Route 9 near Smithville.

To me, bucktailing is a well-nigh perfect way to fish. Success is up to the patience and skill of each individual fisherman, yet anglers share their knowledge and help the tyro get over the hump of catching his first few fish. There is definitely a lot of personal fishing skill involved when the fish are "off their feed," but this happens so seldom in the spring, given good weather, that most fairly competent anglers get their share of the fish and the satisfaction without suffering the deep frustration that some other forms of striper fishing inflict on anglers.

Bucktailing is an art, easily learned, and once learned not easily forgotten. There must be many other areas similar to the central New Jersey shore where these wonderful lures, used as I have described, should reap a bountiful harvest of fish.

9 / Bass Plugging from Boats

It is perhaps unfortunate that the public image of a boat caster after striped bass is that of a nautical hot-rodder who comes charging up to a good striper spot at high speed, fires off a few casts before his wake has dissipated against the not-distant shore, and then goes roaring off to another spot if his first casts do not raise fish.

This charge-in-and-shoot syndrome is the result of the crowding of boats on good striper spots, and the understandable if not forgivable urge that some anglers have to grab fish before the other fellow can get his licks. Fortunately, the majority of skilled boat casters look at their sport through different eyes.

The primary aim of any real casting expert is to fish a good spot undisturbed by other boats, and to make his approach as quietly as possible so as not to spook the fish before he has had a chance to test them out with his plugs. Here's the system I use when I have decided to cast over a promising rocky reef.

First, I have done my homework and determined when to be there to take advantage of a favorable phase of the tide. Morning and evening twilight is usually best, but I have done a lot of good casting during the middle of the day after the mob has gone home for lunch. When I reach the vicinity of my chosen spot I very often troll around a bit if other boats are present, waiting for them to go away. Eventually when the other boats have left I ease my boat inshore toward the rocky reef or headland I want to explore. I do so at slow trolling speed, not changing the

sound field of the boat, but during the drift it doesn't seem to make much difference whether I shut off the motor or let the engine idle in neutral.

As I ease in toward the reef, I carefully calculate the combined wind and current drift. I position the boat up-drift of the reef so the drift of the boat will put me within easy casting range of the prime portions of the reef. These spots vary in position from reef to reef, but usually lie along the offshore axis of the reef and the down-tide slope of this axis.

My tackle usually consists of a fairly stiff surf spinning rod balanced to 20 pound test line, equipped with a boat rod butt and universal butt-end gimbal fitting. Many boat casters prefer "conventional" tackle, in which case 36-pound test braided casting line is best. Hanging from a wooden dowel under the cockpit side covering board is a selection of plugs. There are five basic types of plugs used for stripers and they can be defined about as follows:

Popper—a tail-heavy floating plug with a dished or concave front end designed to splash or "pop" when the line is jigged energetically with the rod. It is a surface attractor depending on noise to attract fish, and is good for rough, dirty water and when bait is active on the surface.

Darter—a floating plug with a long, sloping surface cut into the top of the front end that makes the plug dart erratically from side to side as it is retrieved with moderate rod action. It is good for calm water and slight to moderate chop and is mainly a clear water visual fish attractor.

Swimmer—a floating or sinking plug with an adjustable front nose plate or lip that causes the plug to undulate or "swim" as it is trolled or retrieved at moderate speed. It is a good all-purpose plug when stripers are deep. It resembles whiting, mullet, mackerel, squid, and other bait fish.

Diver—a floating or sinking plug, usually long and slim, that has a long nose lip to force the plug to dive deeply when trolled or retrieved at constant speed. It is

very useful when large fish are laying quite deep and one does not want to resort to wire line or trolling sinkers.

Countdown plug—a relatively new development. This sinking plug has a known rate of sink, making it possible to predetermine its working depth by a careful mentally timed countdown. It is usually rigged to swim at the level at which the retrieve is started.

The first drift is usually the most important one and seems to set the stage for whatever happens afterward. I personally prefer to start off with a fairly noisy

His and hers on popping plugs in a quiet Cape Cod cove.

plug on the theory that by waking the fish up to a new situation I'll get action more quickly. Therefore, I bend a popper onto the leader if there is the least suggestion of ripple or chop on the surface. If the water is dead calm I usually start out with a swimmer or a darter.

I match the plug's color to the immediate water situation. For example, I like to use a dark mackerel-finish plug on days when there is a dark sky heavily lined with clouds. If the water has color from beach sand and sediment, I choose a light-

Left to right, these favorite plugs are: Creek Chub Jointed Pikie, Arbogast Dasher, Mirro-Lure, Creek Chub Striper Strike, Atom Striper Strike, Stan Gibbs Darter, Yellow-silver Rebel.

Work the Gibbs Darter very slowly and easily.

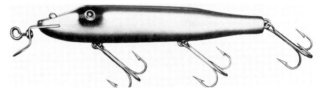

The Creek Chub Pikie can be cast or trolled.

Rebel plugs are effective floater-divers.

Pop the Striper Strike fast and hard.

er-colored plug with some yellow on it, or white-and-red. At night I use either very dark or very light colors. In bright sunlight with very clear water, I prefer medium-dark plugs with a few bright accent spots of contrasting color.

I almost always make my casts withdrift and down-wind, and I don't try to cast a country mile. I keep the casts within 60 to 75 feet of the boat, because it is very important to observe how the stripers rise to and follow the plug as you

drift over and cast over a chosen spot. Beginning casters invariably spot only the most obvious rises and follows. The eye requires considerable training to spot the faint boil a foot or two behind a plug that indicates where a bass has risen almost to the surface and then turned cautiously away before making contact.

The importance of being able to observe and identify these rises is that they help to prove that stripers are present. If the first drift or two gets a number of rises and follows, but no actual hits, a smart caster will soon figure out how to entice the fish into making the last, strike-producing effort. This may be a change in plug type, a change in retrieve tactics, or a combination of both.

When the drift is obviously over, I motor at slow speed back to the original starting point, or possibly to a different starting point that will give me a different drift covering an unexplored portion of the reef. Here I have to use caution in making my decision. If I have had hits or rises and follows on the first drift, it would be silly not to re-work that fishy area on the theory that once the resident fish have been aroused, they may easily be stimulated into striking action on subsequent drifts.

On the other hand, if the drift has been an inshore one and has produced no visible action, a fresh drift further offshore with deep-swimming or deep-darting plugs may locate fish that, for some reason, have chosen to lie in water deeper than usual.

From this discussion we can see that the success of striped bass plug casting from boats usually depends on four major factors. These are:

1. Predicting when to visit a known productive spot when the phase of the tide and the existing wind and sea pattern will be favorable and there will be little competition from other boats. This requires local knowledge.

2. Sizing up the local water color and surf situation so as to make a proper choice of plugs.

3. Covering the drift area with a pattern of casts that will excite and arouse the resident fish without alarming them.

4. Being able to read signs of rises and follows that indicate the first, tentative interest of resident fish in your plugs, and then adapting techniques and fresh lures to raise this interest on the part of the fish to the striking level.

In the casting situation below, a tidal current flows from top to bottom along a rocky shore with an onshore breeze. The boat starts a slow power move at "A", powering down-tide while casting downwind to the rocky areas inshore. At "B" the boat starts a drift. Wind and current combine to drift it to "C". If fish are raised anywhere between "A" and "C", the boat returns up-tide and up-wind to rework the good location. If not, it begins a slow power move at "C" toward "D", working over the last good casting areas with the plugs and lures. The boat stays outside the 12-foot depth line.

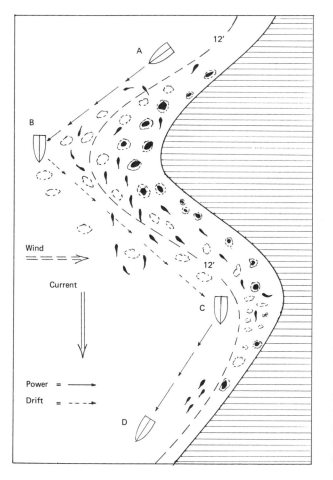

Success also depends upon mental attitude. Plug casting puts you on very intimate terms with the fish and makes the connection between yourself and the fish a rather personal matter. It is surprisingly easy to psyche yourself into a frame of mind that is actually destructive to good fishing. For example, when I first started bass fishing many years ago I had a run of bad luck. For a while I was always the last one to get in on a blitz, the first one to quit and go home when I should have stuck it out, the slowest to solve the riddle of how to convert rises and follows into strikes.

It got so bad that I finally found myself actually taking perverse pride in my ability not to catch stripers. Fortunately, I got in with an old timer who recognized my symptoms and took the trouble to straighten me out. Once, when I was out with him in his boat, I started to reel in fast after making only part of a retrieve. The old guy sidled over and stepped heavily on my toes. While I was hopping around on one foot, cussing him for his clumsiness, a fish hit my motionless plug.

He didn't have to step on my foot the second time to prove the point that you can't *force* stripers onto the hook, but you can *entice* them by taking it slow and easy. This, of course, requires a relaxed, positive-thinking attitude. Now, whenever I go striper fishing, I spend a little time psyching myself into the correct frame of mind. Believe me, it works.

• I *know* there are fish out there to be caught.

• I *know* my tackle is good.

• I *know* that if the fish won't respond to one tactic, they will eventually respond to another.

Finally, even if I don't catch fish, I *know* that it's because the fish have a lot to say about how the fishing goes. I know I can't always win and that a fishless day is no eternal stain upon my soul. I know that my patience is greater than theirs, and I

Here a submerged reef with projecting rocks lies off a sharp headland. The current flows toward the reef as shown by arrows. The breeze blows approximately opposite to the current, setting up a rip front on the up-tide edge of the reef. The boat starts at "A", powering slowly up-tide to cast up-wind at "B" and "C" along the rip. If no fish are found in the rip, the boat makes a power-assisted drift stern-first through the passage from "D" to "E". It then continues the power-assisted drift from "E" through "F" and "G" back to "A". From "E" to "G" the casting is down-wind while the drift is over shallow water.

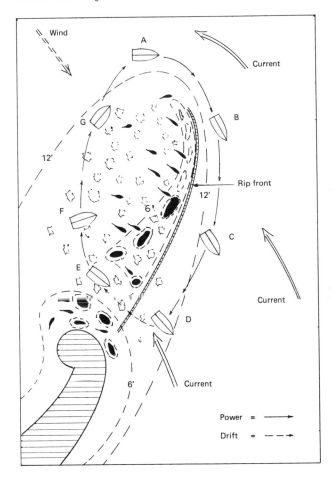

The high control seat on this Old Town stern-drive boat is excellent for spotting rocks and fish in restricted waters such as this Maine cove.

know that they cannot lay down there in the water scheming to outwit me the way I plan and scheme to outwit them.

Because plug casting for stripers is so often done very close to the shore, an element of danger often creeps into the fishing. The best fishing often happens when there is a swell running or a fairly strong onshore wind and chop. No plug caster in his right mind ever works near the beach without a good anchor and line ready in the bow of the boat. And he is careful not to put spare gear on top of the line where it can foul up the quick use of the ground tackle in an emergency.

The emergency is usually failure of the motor just when you need it most in a tight pinch in a rough sea, failure of steer-ing gear under extreme pressure, or failure of the people in the boat to spot and react to a bigger-than-usual swell or growler that is sure to break offshore of them.

A well-handled boat can survive a surprising amount of heavy surf provided the passengers don't fall down and break an arm or leg, or get tossed overboard. In some instances it is actually possible for a small boat to stay inside the first line of breakers and ride out the bad seas in the foam between breaking surf and beach until the seas subside enough to make possible a dash to safety in deep water. But taking care not to get caught inside of a breaking sea is better strategy.

The steering gear should be very strong

and should be inspected at frequent intervals for signs of wear. Look for "burrs" on steering cables where they pass through sheaves or fairleads. A burred cable should be replaced at once. Look to make sure that the bolts or screws holding sheaves in place have not corroded or become loose in the boat's wood or fiberglass. Don't store gear under the after deck where it can roll or shift into a position that will jam the steering quadrant.

Make sure that the engine always responds instantly to a touch on the starter button, and that the batteries are always up. Having two batteries, one for the engine and one for radio, lights, sounder, etc., is a good idea. If the boat has only one alternator or generator, install a double-diode dual battery control system that will charge either or both batteries on demand from the single generator without discharging the opposite battery through use of lights, sounder, etc.

It is no longer considered sissy to wear a life preserver when fishing in potentially dangerous waters. The new flotation wind-breaker jackets available at many sport clothing shops make good sense. The boat itself should have enough flotation in the form of plastic foam blocks fastened or poured into the hull to support the hull and passengers if a breaking sea fills the hull with water. If this should ever happen to you, *stay with the boat!* Don't attempt to swim ashore to get help.

For the striped bass enthusiast who is sick of the old trolling routine and wants to develop his personal fishing skill, plug casting from small boats is a logical step forward. The boat does not have to be expensive, the tackle is simple, and the fishing can be highly satisfying. It is not a style of fishing that every beginner should try. But once a man or woman has mastered the fundamentals, few other fishing techniques can put him or her on such an intimate level with these wonderful fish.

Captain Ralph Gray took this 68-pounder on a popping plug, fishing from a small outboard boat off the ocean beach near the outer tip of Cape Cod.

YOU DON'T HAVE TO BE A DOCTOR TO CATCH fish, but it often helps if you have a supply of surgical tubing. With simple modifications, this simple medical supply becomes one of the hottest striped bass lures, a fish-catching device that has withstood the test of time. What's more, this is a lure you can make yourself in a number of successful configurations.

The surgical tubing lure boasts four distinct advantages over large spoons or trolling plugs: (1) You achieve more hook-ups, (2) you lose fewer fish after they are hooked, (3) the stripers fight harder without a large, rigid artificial lure in their mouths, and (4) you can cut and rig tubes to fish for just about any size of stripers from "rats" just over the legal size to trophy fish over 50 and 60 pounds.

Although it is easy to cut a length of rubber or plastic tubing and put a hook in the tail end, the most successful tube users have a bag full of tricks based on constant experimentation. It takes only an extra moment or so to apply these tricks, provided you know them.

I got my introduction to tube lure lore from Capt. Joe Renzo of Highlands, N. J. Joe knows as much about surgical tubing lures as any man fishing for stripers. History is clouded, but the tube lure has been traced back to the 1940's when it was first used off Sandy Hook, N. J. A handful of local experts carefully guarded their knowledge as they hauled in heavyweight stripers in the currents and rips that mark the entrance to New York Harbor. Now, in the 1970's, the tube lure is firmly established from the mid-Atlantic to Cape Cod as one of the top striper producers.

Surgical and light industrial tubing is available from a number of supply houses. It comes in large spools and you can buy a whole spool or any number of feet of tubing. Some tackle wholesalers supply tubing in popular sizes and colors, selling it by the yard. The best diameters vary from ¼ inch to ½ inch and you should select several grades of wall thickness for your own experimentation.

Tube lures are cut into two major length ranges. Short tubes six to eight inches long are used on smaller bass while "snakes" from 16 inches to 24 inches long take the toll of the larger fish. The shorter tubes have greater rigidity and are inclined to spin. Long tubes can be adjusted to simulate the slow, snake-like sweeping action of a natural eel. Each type of action seems to appeal to the fish.

Unroll a length of tubing and look at it closely. The most desirable lures are cut from portions that have a natural curve with a lazy "S" turn being the optimum. Don't throw away perfectly straight sections of tubing. These can be fixed. A single-curve tube lure resembles a thin new moon crescent while the desired "S" turn combination looks like two crescent moons joined end to end and facing in opposite directions.

To construct a tube in the larger length class, measure the tubing, paying particular attention to the natural curve. Snip out the measured section with a pair of sharp scissors. It should not be under 15 inches

10 / Those Marvelous Tube Lures

long and usually will average 18 inches to 20 inches.

Select the end with the less pronounced curve for the tail end. Mark the tubing at a point two inches from the end of the tail. With your sharp scissors, make a diagonal cut from the mark to the end of the tail. Now here's the rub. You must start the cut from the *inside* of the tube's curvature, working toward the *outside* as you cut toward the tail end. This is extremely important for preserving the proper action of the lure.

You have the option of rigging a one- or two-hook lure, with the single-hook-in-tail being the preferred method. The tail hook varies in size from 5/0 to 7/0, depending on the size of the stripers you expect to encounter. The O'Shaughnessy pattern seems to have a slight edge over other styles.

Using two pairs of pliers, twist open the eye of the hook, insert one end ring of a barrel swivel, then twist the hook eye closed. Select a swivel that will fit snugly inside the tubing. It should have a breaking test of at least 50 pounds.

Where the possibility exists that you may hook big bluefish or other sharp-toothed critters, use flexible nylon-covered stranded wire leader. Otherwise,

Made of easily obtained surgical rubber tubing, the tube lure resembles a sand eel or large spearing in the water.

monofilament of 40 to 50 pounds test is good. To make up a single-hook rig, cut a length of leader longer than the tubing by at least a foot. Fasten the leader to the barrel swivel and then pass the leader up from the tail end through the tube, using an eel-rigging needle. Pull the hook swivel up into the tube until the hook eye is snug against the tubing at its diagonally cut end.

The tandem-hook tube rig is accom-

plished in much the same manner, but with a simple trick that helps tremendously. First, the forward hook should be two sizes smaller than the tail hook. Thus, a 7/0 tail hook should have a 5/0 hook for its head mate. When rigged, the smaller hook should be placed so that the swivel attached to its eye is just inside the head of the tube. The head end is cut square across the tubing.

To accomplish this, attach the swivels

Cut the tail end at an angle, starting the cut on the inside of the natural curve of the tube. Thread the leader through the tubing with an eel-rigging needle. The essential parts are cheap and easy to obtain.

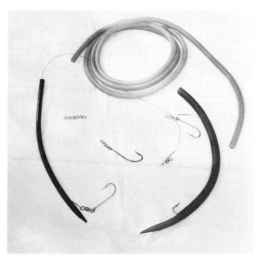

to the hooks and the leader to the tail hook. Then lay the tube flat on a smooth surface and place the head hook at the head end of the tubing, the back of the hook against the inside of the tube's curvature. Adjust the hook and the swivel so the swivel is exactly where it would be when snugly inserted in the tube end. Then mark the spot where the hook bend will emerge from the tube wall, on the inside of the tube curvature.

With a sharp knife point, make a small hole at this spot. Now, starting at the tail end of the tube, thread the leader up through the tube and out through this small hole. Tie the end of the leader to the eye of the swivel that is in the head hook eye, making the leader exactly long enough to permit the swivel and hook to be inserted into the head end of the tube via the small hole. If there is doubt in your mind as to the precise length, leave the leader slightly slack.

Finally, insert the swivel and head hook into the tube head end via the small hole. The tandem rig is now complete. Pull the swivel up into the head end so that just the upper swivel eye protudes from the tube. You can store the tube lure as is in the tackle box. When you are ready to go fishing, attach a three to four foot section of 50 or 60 pound test leader to the exposed eye of the head swivel.

If the tubing is straight and lacks the action-giving curve, the identical procedure is carried out with one important exception. When you tie the head hook swivel to the leader, make the leader an inch or so shorter than the length of the tubing between the hooks. This will automatically cause the tube to assume a curve when the head hook is inserted into the tube's upper end.

Some tube makers use bead chain swivel for the head swivel, or attach a bead chain swivel snap to the end of the fishing line. Soft lines sometimes tend to twist up badly with some tube lures unless a keel sinker is attached between line and leader. Here, a monofilament leader 12 to 15 feet long is not too long. Wire trolling line strongly resists twisting and a sinker should not be necessary if you use the tube lure with wire line.

The eel-like action of tube lures can often be improved by inserting a small block-tin casting jig into the head end. Experimentation is required to come up with the right combination of head weight, head bend, and retrieve speed to create the desired action.

The best way to test a tube lure is to snap it onto a light spinning rig and make a few casts and retrieves in clear water. As you reel in, watch how the tube acts. Metal squids have a hook molded into the tail end of the jig. Cut the hook off with a hacksaw and dress the tail end with a file until it is a snug fit for the tube. The easy way to attach the tube leader to the squid is as follows:

Pull the leader up through the tube and don't attach a swivel or head hook to its upper end. Instead, shove the dressed end of the squid into the tube, allowing the leader to protrude. Pass the leader

A super-eel made of tubing may be up to 24 inches long with at least two hooks.

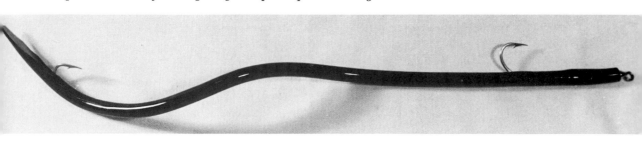

through the eye of the squid and then tie on the swivel, outside the squid eye. This puts all the weight of a fish directly on the leader from swivel to tail hook.

Metal squids often need bending or shaping. Lead jigs break when pressure is applied to them, but jigs cast from block tin can be bent between the fingers to give the side-to-side sweeping action that imitates the natural eel as it swims.

There are many ways to enhance the fishability of tube lures. Surgical tubing usually comes in a light tan color, but a quick dip in a simple dye like Tintex can change the color in moments. Dark red or black tubes seem to work well on big stripers, especially at night. Joe Renzo claims that the mark of the successful tube fisherman is willingness to experiment with lure color and action, trolling depth, and trolling speed. He insists that not only do stripers change preferences from day to day, they often change from tide to tide.

Long tubes should be trolled at the slowest speed that will impart action. If one speed fails to produce strikes, try another. When boats in your area are taking fish with identical lures, and you are not, try to match speed exactly with the successful ones. Line length may also be critical, especially when you are using trolling sinkers or wire line to get down deep.

Many small boat owners rig a pair of surf rods wing-and-wing from cockpit rod holders to simulate miniature outriggers. Keel sinkers will range from an ounce or two where there is little tide to six or eight ounces for places where the tide is very strong. Because boats often have to run faster in order to maintain headway in strong tidal currents, some canny tube artists save their tubes for the slower currents of tide just before and after high or low water slack.

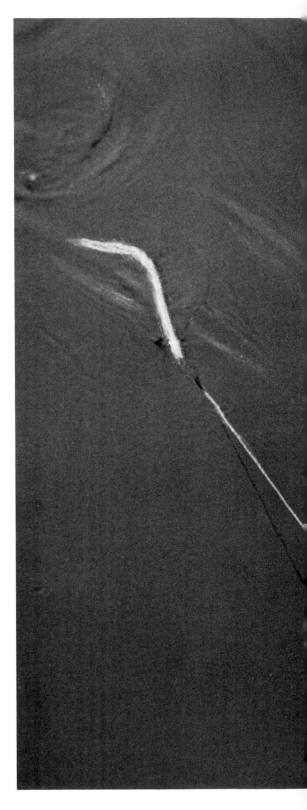

When towed slowly the tube lure should show eel-like motion.

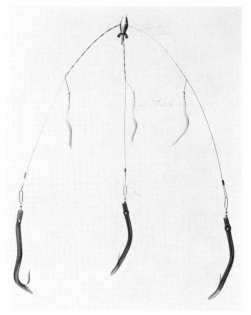

The so-called "umbrella frame rig" is a wire frame attached to a lead towing head. Two or more tube lures may be attached to each wire arm, resembling a small school of bait fish when trolled.

Short tube lures are often very deadly on school stripers. They are simple to make. Cut the tubing in six to eight inch lengths and make a diagonal two inch tail cut on the inside of the curve as before. Take a long-shank hook of the proper size (5/0 to 7/0), attach a suitable swivel to the hook eye and a length of leader to the other eye of the swivel. Haul the swivel and hook snugly up into the tube until the bend of the hook is flush with the upper end of the diagonal tail cut. Some anglers thread a bright-colored streamlined plastic bead onto the leader at this point and force the bead down into the head end of the tube for a "nose."

If action is not sufficient, bend the shank of the hook about 30° to impart the desired spinning or twisting motion. Short tubes that spin hard twist lines, even those of spinning tackle in casting. For extended trolling, they must be used with keel sinkers to save the lines.

The so-called umbrella rig that became popular at a few ports back in 1969 seems to be an adaption of the West Coast dropper rig. West Coast striper fishermen for a number of years have been using a two-lure rig devised from a "Y"-shaped piece of springy wire. Leaders are attached to each end of the "Y" so that two lures can be trolled from one fishing line.

As developed at Montauk and other ports in 1969 and 1970, the umbrella rig is an "X" frame of crossed wires from which four or more tube lures can be trolled at the same time. What this contraption looks like to the fish, I'd hesitate to guess, but it works surprisingly well, despite its ungainly appearance. Unfortunately, the multi-hook umbrella rig is not recognized by the IGFA as "legal" tackle, so if a record is your aim, stick to baits or lures that won't cause your hard-won trophy striper to be disqualified at the last heart-breaking moment.

The tube striper rig is one of those rare things, a type of lure that offers an almost infinite variety of attractive, fish-catching lures that can be made from inexpensive, easily obtained materials. Use the suggestions given here as a springboard for developing your own "secret weapon" striper lures.

OLD TIMERS IN THE STRIPED BASS FRATERNITY agree that one natural bait lure outshines all others when it comes to nailing big stripers. This super-bait is the lowly black eel. More big fish have been caught on rigged natural eels than on any other single natural or artificial casting or trolling bait or lure. The wonderful thing about eels is that they can be used either for casting or trolling without much change of rigging, once you understand what it is about eels that stripers like.

As Al Reinfelder explains elsewhere in this book in his chapter on rigging and using artificial plastic eels, the real secret of using any eel—natural or artificial—is to move the eel through the water at a speed that gives the eel natural swimming action. You can do this by trolling or by reeling-in after casting the eel from shore or from a boat. In either case the effect has to be the same. The eel must look natural and alive in the water to attract the attention of a big striper.

Depth, stability, and swimming action is provided by a metal head jig to which the head of the eel is carefully fastened. There are many models of head jigs, some more effective than others. If you know a man who owns a mold for casting superior eel head jigs, love that man like a brother. Buy him beer. Treat him to steak. Cozen him with sweet words. Maybe he'll sell or lend you a few good head jigs. Otherwise, you'll have to make do with the "store-boughten" variety available at most striper-area tackle stores.

The best head jigs are cast of a mixture of lead and tin (the best are pure tin) that permits you to bend and shape the jig body without breaking it. With the exception of a very few superior jigs, most head jigs need a wee bit of bending to attain just the right kind of side-to-side swimming motion. This is because natural eels vary in length, weight, and pliability. Manufactured plastic eels have one big advantage, that of uniform shape, size, and pliability.

The best eels range from 12 to 16 or even 18 inches long and are thin rather than thick. The head jig has a fixed hook of at least 6/0 size, plus a small auxiliary brass stub or hole drilled in the body, to which the tail hook lashing line is made fast. The eel is rigged as shown in the illustrations accompanying this chapter.

Don't try to use monofilament for the tail hook. It is difficult to tie, and its stiffness detracts from the eel's natural pliability. The very best line is old-fashioned Cuttyhunk linen fishing line in sizes of 24-thread (72 pound test) or larger. Unfortunately, this is now hard to come by. Many anglers use last season's 80 pound test Dacron tuna line. Fifty pound test line is about the lightest you should use for the eel tail hook.

Once you have a supply of eels made up, you can store them in packages of two or three in your freezer. They keep indefinitely. In the field they keep very well without refrigeration if packed in coarse Kosher salt, but salt has a tendency to corrode even the best plated hooks. You can re-freeze eels without hook problems if

11 / Rigging and Using the Striper Eel

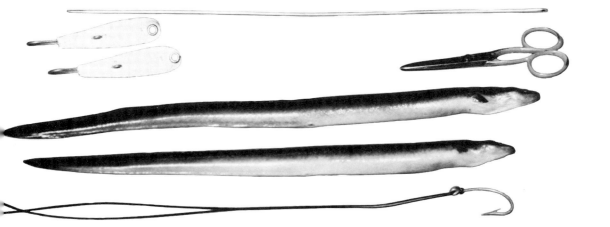

Provide eels, long needle, head jigs, scissors, 7/o hook snelled with a piece of doubled 80-pound Dacron line.

Run needle through body from behind the vent to the mouth. Hook ends of tail hook line into eye of needle.

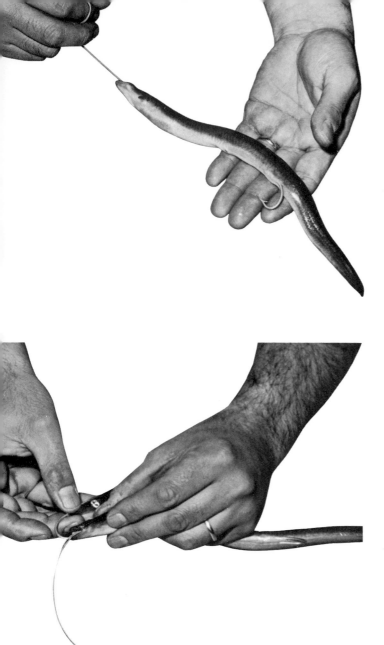

Pull tail hook line up through the eel's body, drawing shank of the hook well up into meat of the tail.

Take the head jig and pass the point of its hook into the eel's mouth to a spot back of the eel's eyes.

Push point and bend of head jig hook out through top of eel's head, keeping end of jig inside mouth.

Knot ends of tail hook over the anchor pin cast into body of head jig; tie so they won't slip.

Using ends of tail hook line or a separate piece of line, wrap and tie the eel's mouth around end of jig.

Here are three variations of the rigged eel, showing relative positions of the head jig and tail hook.

you wash them in fresh water before re-freezing.

The eel is basically a twilight or night-time lure. The term "lure" is proper here because despite its natural origin, the eel is rigged and used as a lure rather than a dead or live bait.

The best trolling speed is quite slow, often not more than 1½ or two m.p.h., but you have to test each eel for the speed that produces the best undulating action. Some may require a little more or less speed than others. Try to use eels that call for about the same speed when you are trolling two or more lines.

Test each eel by holding the rod tip down close to the water with the eel visible underwater, close to the stern, on a very short line. The swimming should be slow and snake-like, not fast and frantic. Forget everything you have ever read about "beautiful, frantic bait-fish action" when you fish with eels. Stripers go for slow, lazy-swimming eels. A frantically swimming or spinning eel may get bluefish hits, but stripers will ignore it.

When the eel is swimming properly you should be able to feel the swimming action with the tip of your rod as a sort of rhythmic, regular pulsation. Learn to relate this feel to the appearance of the swimming eel as you test the eel before putting it out full distance. If the eel suddenly goes "dead," it's a sure sign that one of the hooks has picked up seaweed or the eel's tail has somehow come around and hooked onto the tail hook. The only remedy is to pull it in and correct the condition.

Eels are bottom-dwelling creatures and the best place to fish them is close to the bottom. This may require the use of a trolling sinker or wire line. If you prefer to use mono or Dacron line for IGFA reasons, give the eel a leader of 60 pound test monofilament at least 12 feet, but not over 15 feet long. A four-ounce trolling sinker between line and leader will add about six feet to the depth of the eel with 100 feet of soft line out. Without a drail, the eel should swim at a depth of about four feet. So the four-ounce sinker puts it down to about ten feet at normal trolling speed.

Wire line will sink a trolled eel at a length-depth ratio of about 8:1. Thus, 100 feet of wire will put the eel down to a trolling depth of about 12 feet. As in other types of deep trolling, an electronic depth finder is very helpful.

When fishing eels in the surf, it pays to take your time on the retrieve. The surf angler has more opportunity than the boat troller to give variety to the action of the eel. Here, again, you have to learn to judge the slight pulsating action of the rod when the eel is swimming properly. With too slow a retrieve the eel head jig might take the eel down into rocks where it will find a permanent home. Too fast a retrieve will not get hits.

The ideal surf casting retrieve is a moderately slow reeling pace occasionally broken by a long, slow lift of the rod tip followed by a few seconds' pause to allow the eel to sink toward the bottom. This undulating, up-and-down swimming action is very effective on big bass.

Surf men use eels mainly at twilight and during the night. Good locations are beside big rocks that cause discolored boils on a generally sandy beach, over rocky and ledgy bottom, off harbor breakwaters, and at the mouths of small guts or tidal streams that connect inshore bays or salt ponds with the ocean or large bodies of water.

Success with eels comes from practice, but the tools for rigging eels are simple, and they are not at all hard to learn to rig. Once mastered, the rigged eel is the striper addict's most potent big-bass weapon.

12 / When Bait is Best

SOME FISHERMEN HAVE BEEN CONDITIONED TO believe that the pinnacle of achievement is to take a good fish on an artificial lure, but experienced striper anglers know that the time always comes when bait is best. They also realize that bait fishing is no shortcut to success. A successful bait fisherman is every bit as worthy of acclaim when he makes an outstanding catch as is the man or woman who sticks to artificials.

Natural bait for stripers falls into two major categories, dead and alive, and into several classes under each category. Types employed include herring, mackerel, clams, worms, eels, menhaden, squid, crabs, and shrimp. In fresh water such delicacies as crayfish, baby sunfish, shad, shiners, and suckers have been used successfully.

Herring. This heading should also include alewives and river-run shad on the way from salt water to spawn. Springtime is usually the best time to use these members of the herring family, and many anglers collect their live baits by hand or dipnet in small streams used by the fish for spawning. The fish must be put into water tanks or GI cans full of water immediately to survive alive, although dead whole herring, alewives, or shad often attract large stripers when fished on or near the bottom in tidewater.

A live herring, shad, or alewife is hooked lightly through the back, usually with one prong of a 4/0 or 5/0 treble hook placed under the skin just behind the dorsal fin. Another good way to live-hook a herring is to slip the point of an 8/0 O'Shaughenessy hook up through the upper lip, leaving the mouth and lower jaw free for water intake to the gills.

Herring, shad, and alewives attract medium to big stripers when fished in bays, sounds, river mouths, or estuaries into which the bait fish move in the spring, seeking fresh water creeks and rivers for spawning. Cape Cod Canal is a great place for this kind of live-lining. Best fishing is usually at morning or evening twilight and after dark, although fine catches can be made during daylight hours when bait is available.

Some anglers use a short shock-leader of 40 or 50 pound test monofilament, but many experts prefer to tie the 20 or 30 pound test mono fishing line directly to the hook. The bait is allowed to swim free. When a big bass zeros in on the herring, the bait usually becomes quite active before the bass takes it, often forewarning the angler of impending action. When a pickup is felt, the angler must resist the impulse to strike.

The fish should be allowed to swim off with the bait in its mouth, the reel in free-spool and only very light fingertip pressure on the spool to prevent a backlash. Eventually the striper will stop to maul the bait a bit and finally swallow it. When you feel the fish swimming off the second time, this is the time to strike the hook into the striper. A big striper may rip off as much as 100 yards of line after being struck, so the reel must have very good capacity.

Bait fishing is one of the oldest methods of angling and often works when artificial lures fail to attract fish, but bait must be used with knowledge and skill.

A good tackle combination for live herring, mackerel, eels, or similar good sized bait is a medium surf casting rod designed for 20 to 30 pound test line, mounting a level-wind, star drag reel with a capacity of at least 300 yards of line. A similar trolling rod will work well, although some anglers prefer a trolling rod in the 30 to 50 pound line class for its heavier backbone when dealing with the big stripers that may rock up in rough bottom.

Mackerel. In northeastern waters, Boston mackerel are prime bait for very large stripers. Small boats are used and the mackerel are obtained by bait or jig fishing in deeper water outside the 'long-shore bars behind which the big stripers love to hide. Mackerel are stored in sea water in GI cans or wash tubs, unless the boat has a real live bait well.

Back inside the bar, or over the chosen reef, the boat drifts or is anchored and the mackerel are hooked lightly through the dorsal meat and skin just ahead of the dorsal fin. Each bait is allowed to swim free, but some anglers control depth by means of a split cork put onto the fishing line the desired distance up from the hook. A 4/o or 5/o treble or 7/o to 8/o Eagle Claw hook is favored. The hook is usually tied directly to the line, which may be monofilament testing from a high of 30 pound down to a low of about 12, depending on how big the fish are and how bait-shy they appear to be.

It's important to put only healthy mackerel into the fish tank. Bleeders quickly contaminate the water and cause healthy mackerel to die. Change the water often, or keep a steady stream of clean sea water flowing in from an electric pump. You can aerate an automobile or beach buggy tank by filling a purged LP gas container with high pressure air at a gas station, and bleeding a little air continuously into the bottom of the tank via a valve and air hose. Even an extra spare tire will hold enough air to aerate a 40 gallon tank for a couple of hours.

Mackerel baits are fished the same way as herring, and the secret of success with any live bait is to wait out the first run without causing the striper to spit out the bait before he's ready to swallow it.

Dead herring and mackerel are often fished whole, on the bottom, for very large stripers. Oddly, a pickup on dead bait calls for a quick strike without prolonged dropback. This may be because the fish presumably has no difficulty in turning the bait for swallowing when it picks the motionless dead bait from the bottom.

Mackerel are usually best during July and August, and the best mackerel fishing hours often are those of midmorning to midafternoon. Because you have to go out to deep water to find the macks, fishing mackerel baits is a boat-fishing job.

Clams. In early spring, when stripers first appear along ocean beaches after the winter layover, they can be taken from the surf by fishing with large baits of whole clam meats. The favorite clam appears to be the surf or skimmer clam with small to medium sized clams fished whole and very large clams fished by the half.

Tackle can be any regular "conventional" or spinning surf outfit with proper terminal equipment. The latter consists of one or more 6/o to 8/o Eagle Claw or O'Shaughnessy hooks on a leader of 40 pound test mono. Many anglers use the slip-sinker or "fish-finder" sinker rig which is rigged in this manner:

Pass the fishing line through the brass eye of a suitable pyramid sinker (four ounces or so), and then attach the connector to which the leader is made fast. When the bait and sinker are cast out, the sinker cannot go farther down than the swivel, but once the sinker is on the bottom, the line is free to move through the sinker-eye as freely as the current or undertow may take it.

You can thus let out line through the sinker eye until the bait is separated from the sinker by a number of feet. This facilitates a quick swallow of the hook when a fish picks up the bait, but it also requires a sensitive hand on the rod to interpret what's going on out there. When you feel the weight of a fish, strike him hard and quickly.

Another entirely different use of clams for stripers is the chumming system developed in Chesapeake Bay and used at a number of locations up and down the East Coast. Clam bellies, obtained in bulk from bait dealers, are run through a grinder to render them down to soup. The boat anchors at a favorable location and starts chumming with this clam soup mixed with sea water. Baits of small, hard pieces of clam foot are used, although many anglers prefer casting and retrieving diamond or bucktail jigs.

Mass chumming with clams by fleets of boats has proved extremely effective near Chesapeake Bay Bridge and at Montauk Point, N.Y. The clam soup apparently works the fish up to a high pitch of hunger without giving them much to chew on. One problem has been the fact that chummers do not like trolling boats moving into their chum lines, and nasty situations have occasionally developed over who has the "right" to fish a given patch of striper water.

Milt Rosko (above) likes a gob of blood worms for stripers from the beach.

Spearing, sand eels, and silversides are prime bait for school stripers.

Worms. For school fish in the spring, it's hard to beat blood or sand worms in some localities. Take the entrance to Shrewsbury River, behind Sandy Hook, for example. From up inside the bridges to 'way out behind the Hook, you will see literally hundreds of small boats drifting or moving ever so slowly, fishing worms. The tackle is very light and the action is hardly what you'd call a blitz, but at the end of any given day many hundreds of stripers are taken ashore by the fleet.

Worm fishing is a subtle art as any angler will verify who has spent frustrating days dunking worms, watching other happy fishermen haul in stripers all around him while he catches sea weed and a throbbing ulcer. First, the hooks must be small, often as small as size #4. Next, the line must be light. If you think 12 pound test line should be about right, fish with six. If six won't take fish, drop down to four or even three pound line.

Use good, live worms, and fish them slow and easy. Drift if the current is too strong for anchoring. Anchor if the wind is too strong for drifting. Plan in advance to fish when a strong wind is against the tide, slowing your drift or the current to a moderate value. Stripers like current and slowly moving worms, fished near the bottom. Sometimes spinners help, sometimes they seem to scare the fish away. You have to experiment.

For worming I prefer a very light rod, a little longer than a conventional trolling rod, and a small level-wind, star drag reel. Some anglers fish worms very well with spinning tackle. The important point is to use tackle with good "feel" so you can sense each delicate pickup, and each time the worm touches bottom.

Split shot on the line are sometimes necessary. A sliding ball or shot sinker is better when the current is strong. Some anglers fish no lead at all, slowly stripping out line into the tide until 100 yards or more is out. Naturally, when boats are thick this tactic may not work well.

Keep worms in a cool, ventilated place, preferably at about 40° F. They keep best packed in the damp sea weed supplied by the bait house where they are bought. Don't let them lie around in the hot sun.

A few enterprising anglers have discovered that some stripers respond to bottom-bumped artificial plastic worms as greedily as fresh water bass. Bottom-bumping consists of lifting the rod slightly every little while to hop or "bump" the sunken worm along the bottom. Each hop stirs up mud. The best bumping worms have positive-buoyancy tails that wriggle alluringly as they bump. Ordinary nightcrawlers die quickly in salt water, so stick to sand and blood worms when you fish salt water.

Eels. We have dealt with the arts of trolling and casting natural eels elsewhere in this book, so now let us take a quick look at that deadly striper bait, the live eel. Fishing live eels for bait is a bit of a specialty. For one thing, not everybody can handle the slippery things without getting nipped or working a hook into

one hand. But the experts who use live eels, especially along such beaches as those of the Rhode Island shore, swear there's nothing to beat them for durability, action, and ability to take the biggest kind of stripers.

The best eels for live bait fishing are not too large. Eels of 12 to 15 inches length are about right, with skinny eels preferred over fat ones. You can keep eels alive for days in a container of seaweed wet down with seawater. Freezing will kill them, of course, as will heat. Some anglers catch their own in eel pots, but most purchase their eels alive at bait shops.

Tackle is similar to that used for herring, mackerel, and other live bait, despite the fact that eels are not very bulky. The single hook, usually 4/o to 6/o in size, is inserted under the back skin a little forward of amidships, or through the upper lip and nose. Held in the air and dangling helplessly, the eel will almost invariably try to wrap itself around the line. But in the water it quickly straightens out.

The best eel-fishing spots are over rocky bottom not far from shore. You may have to cork the line to keep the eel out of the rocks, or hold it short above the bottom with a thumb on the spool. The striper strike is usually not at all tentative on an eel and about half of the bass will hook themselves at the first try. When this happens there is no need for a further dropback.

But if you have a strike and then a spit-out, and can still feel the eel struggling on the hook, let the eel swim naturally and give the striper or his friend a chance to come back for a second try. If the pickup is slow and tentative, let the fish swim the bait away and eat it before striking the hook home.

Johnny Kronuch contemplates a pugnacious crab that will soon be striper bait.

A small live or dead herring, hooked through the lips, makes a fine bait for very big stripers.

The best eeling time is in the fall, from twilight through night-time to dawn. Occasionally eels take big fish in daylight hours. Because of the danger of abrasion against rocks, some anglers put the eel hook on a shock leader of mono at least ten pounds heavier in test than the fishing line.

Menhaden. Fishing with snag-hooked live menhaden was described in the opening chapter of this book. Nowadays, anglers in the Sandy Hook area and a few other regions are able to buy live menhaden, or bunkers, from bait dealers who get them from fish traps or bunker seine boats. Menhaden are large bait, but keep fairly well in a large bait well that is liberally supplied with water.

At Sandy Hook, where a big menhaden-fishing fleet gathers in August, September, and October, these big baits are fished on tackle of up to 50 pound line test. Best results, however, are said to be had on lighter line. The herring-mackerel terminal rig is used, with the hook going into the bunker's back just ahead of the dorsal fin, or under the tip of its nose and out through the upper lip.

Menhaden are strong fish and a large split cork is often necessary on the line to keep them from diving into rocks or kelp patches. A long, controlled drop-back is a must after the strike, and it is not uncommon for the striper to take out more than 50 yards of line on the first easy run after the pickup. Stripers appear to munch or "scale" menhaden before eating them, and many a good fish is lost because of a premature strike.

In recent years, live menhaden have been snagged by surfcasters using heavy jigs and large treble hooks. This style of fishing has put zing into the late fall surf fishing of the Carolina Outer Banks where finding a way to get the big stripers to strike was, for many years, a tough problem. Lacking menhaden, the fish often will take small weakfish, porgies, or whiting.

Squid. By itself, squid is not often used as striper bait unless an angler cannot find other natural bait more to his liking. But narrow strips of fresh squid are very excellent additions to trolled striper lures. Squid is an important striper food, however, and there is no reason why properly rigged whole squid baits should not prove to be very effective on stripers, especially if they are fished deep on wire line or by means of downriggers.

Crabs. A few anglers have obtained very satisfying results fishing crab baits in inshore areas where the stripers happen to be feeding heavily on such fare. The channels between the grass meadows of the great Long Island and New Jersey wetlands are prime crab-fishing areas. Green crabs, small blue crabs, and large fiddlers are the preferred species.

Shrimp. Northern anglers have had little opportunity to experiment with shrimp for striper bait, largely because northern grass shrimp for years have been in almost non-existant supply. Now, eel grass beds are recovering from a massive blight (to the distress of shoreside householders) and grass shrimp are again becoming plentiful.

Chumming with grass shrimp and baiting with whole, free-swimming shrimp is highly successful on weakfish in the spring and early summer, and may prove equally successful on stripers in wetland and inshore areas where these small shrimp are plentiful.

Bait fishing is very often a welcome change of pace. In some locations it is the preferred method for taking very large fish. In others it is a reliable alternate method when artificials fail. In a few startling instances, it is the only way to rescue success from stripers that have suddenly gone berserk, as they sometimes will, breaking all the rules of normal fish behavior. The smart angler practices the kinds of bait fishing that work in his area against the day when all artificials fail and only bait will do the trick.

The West Coast method of rigging minnows for salmon works equally well when used on striped bass.

The late Al Reinfelder (left) and his partner, Lou Palma, perfected the manufacture and use of a whole new class of artificial eels and lures.

1 3 / How to Fish the Plastic Eel

THE PLASTIC STRIPER EEL IS NOT EXACTLY A new invention. Back in the late 1950's my partner, Lou Palma, and I began experimenting with soft vinyl lures that had the heft and feel of natural eels, yet did not suffer from the eel's need for refrigeration or storage on ice or in coarse salt. The result was a natural-looking, flexible, attractive artificial eel that soon revolutionized bass casting and trolling in many areas.

Soon soft plastic worms, shrimp, baitfish, squid, and other goodies were invading the tackle market. Once anglers learned how to rig and use these realistic lures, game fish were in real trouble. For stripers, the new plastic eels were quite successful. Their built-in swimming action was identical with that of the live eel. Accustomed by nature to look at eels as prime food, the bass soon placed plastic eels high on the list of proven lures.

Fishing the plastic eel successfully, however, is a whole new fishing game. Many anglers never master the relatively simple secrets of using them properly. If you have looked at plastic eels as some far-fetched inventor's dream, or never really caught fish on the eels you've tried, pay close attention while I tell you how they should be used.

The first thing to remember is that the eel bait, whether it's natural or artificial, is primarily an underwater lure. I use the words "bait" and "lure" interchangeably here because it's difficult, with eels, to say when the eel stops being a bait and starts being a lure. Stripers dote on eels and the

eels they catch in the wild are alive. Therefore, if your eel is to be effective, it must simulate the *prime action* of the live eel as closely as possible.

Learning how to achieve prime action is basic to successful eel fishing. Prime action is the swimming motion that most resembles that of a natural live eel. In order to get your plastic eel to perform this way you must know how a live eel swims.

Anquilla rostrata, the American eel, is a snake-like creature that moves through the water in a definitely S-shaped path. Adult eels move at a slow-to-moderate rate, undulating regularly. Young eels wriggle more quickly and tiny elvers (baby eels) move swiftly and erratically. Thus, while all eels swim with the same basic S-motion, size is a major factor in differentiating their various rates of motion.

One of the first things Lou Palma and I learned was that our plastic eels had to "swim" through the water at exactly the same rate of undulation as their live counterparts of the same length and thickness. Believe me, this took some delicate engineering to accomplish! Our "Alou" eels, now manufactured by a major tackle company, are pre-rigged to provide exactly this degree of swimming motion when trolled or retrieved at exactly the proper swimming speed.

The non-success that many fishermen seem to have with plastic eels usually comes from altering the rig to conform with some pet "theory," from re-rigging with homemade heads and other parts, or from trying to make the eel swim too fast through the water.

A properly built plastic eel is equipped with a metal action-head that provides the mechanism to make the eel undulate in a swimming manner when moved through the water. [The same is true with natural eels that are rigged for trolling or casting—Ed.] Each action head is designed to provide the correct built-in action for an eel of a given size. The key is to find the trolling or retrieving speed at which the eel's action starts to kick over.

Cast or troll your eel in clear, quiet water where you can see it clearly. Move it through the water *very slowly.* Then gradually increase the eel's speed. At a given point in speed, the action head will start to move from side to side without spinning, inparting an undulating motion to the plastic eel body. As you increase speed, the action will become more pronounced until it finally becomes frenzied and the eel starts spinning instead of undulating.

Prime action is the action you get at the slowest speed at which the eel swims in the desired S-manner.

This is the retrieve or trolling speed at which the eel will be most effective in attracting and hooking stripers and other game fish. Believe me again when I stress that this is a lot slower than some anglers think. I know because I've sat glued to the bottom in a wet suit for hours, watching the eels swim by. The slower you can work that eel and preserve prime action, the more hits you'll get.

While the principal technique of using a plastic eel is to swim it slowly at a rate designed to develop prime action, when the fish are playing hard-to-get you must be prepared to use special tactics. There are a number of ways in which the basic eel swimming pattern can be varied. One way is to increase the speed of the lure. Do this gradually, for only a slight increase in speed may give the eel the added mo-

tion that it needs to attract fish.

Another type of modified action can be called erratic movement. This does not mean causing the eel to swim in wild jerks and darts. No live eel swims that way. It simply means that the steady trolling or retrieving motion is interrupted at irregular intervals by halts and accelerations.

One of New England's great bass fishermen, a Martha's Vineyard artist, outfishes those around him by simply raising the tip of his rod slightly every five or six seconds as he reels in the eel. Raising and lowering the rod tip while retrieving from a cast, or sweeping the rod fore-and-aft in slow motion while trolling, will cause the eel alternately to rise and dive while swimming. This kind of action is especially attractive to big bass at twilight in clear water.

A very effective way of using plastic eels is to let them scrape or bounce the bottom occasionally. An eel that is pursued by a game fish invariably tries to burrow into the bottom or under rocks for protection. Stripers know this and their feeding or striking instinct seems to be triggered by an eel that occasionally touches or scrapes along the bottom.

Bottom-bouncing in a tide rip may look to the fish like the efforts of a slow-swimming eel to progress up-tide against the strong current. A plastic eel bounced through a hole in the outer bar of an ocean surf may look like an eel actively feeding on worms or sand fleas. When you bounce the eel on bottom, or make it "crawl" over sand, as some anglers are able to do, try to imagine what a live eel would be doing in this particular situation. Then suit your action to the time and place, always remembering that slow-and-easy is better than too fast or too frenzied a type of action.

By relating the specific action of your eel to reasonable natural behavior, you do two things. You increase your own understanding of what fishing is all about while developing the sensitive "feel" for proper fishing action that all good fishermen have to a lesser or greater degree. Don't try to analyze too deeply. Instead, let intuition and hunches lead you on, but don't become hide-bound in your thinking. You have a wonderful fish-computer tucked away between your ears. Let it work for you and you'll catch fish. Save the deep thinking for the nights when you can't fish.

If you are fishing from shore or from a boat that is anchored in a tide-way, cast your eel up-tide so it will be close to hitting bottom by the time it is abreast of you. Raise your rod tip slowly every few moments as you reel in slowly, giving the eel minimum prime action. When you feel a fish pick up the eel, strike him quickly and strongly without waiting to let him get a better grip on the eel. Being plastic, the eel may not taste quite right to him and a quick strike will probably save him.

Natural eels are about the size of a spider's eyelash at birth. Mature eels may reach a length of six feet. You don't need plastic eels to match all the dimensions between these extremes, but certain eel sizes are essential to successful fishing.

When immature eels reach coastal waters from their mid-ocean hatching grounds in the Sargasso Sea, they have just completed the process of pigmentation and are about five inches long. A lure this size is deadly in the early spring.

Female eels seek out coastal rivers which they use as avenues to penetrate hundreds of miles to inland living areas. Males stay along the ocean shore. Young buck "shoestring" eels are extremely appealing to bass of all sizes. New Jersey jetty-jockies rig small eels like these when they can get them in the natural

Joe Pollio gaffs a prime 40-pounder taken on the author's Kuno II *on a plastic eel while trolling in Montauk waters.*

state, and now often prefer the plastic variety because of their availability in tackle shops and durability in use.

Eels 12 to 14 inches long are prime bait for the biggest trophy stripers. At the end of summer, when the stripers are fattening up before the fall migrations, huge eels 18 inches to 20 inches long, sometimes called "Cuttyhunk longfellows," are needed to lure the really large bass. When you switch to eels of a different size, take time to go through the clear-water eel-watching routine again to sharpen your feel for the correct retrieve or trolling speed to make this new size of eel work best.

side. Variations of specific shades, however, are endless. Some natural eels are almost pure black. Others shade through rusty red to washed-out orange, depending on food and environment. Some are grey-green. For these reasons, the most important colors for a fisherman to carry are black, natural grey, grey-green, and amber.

When choosing colors follow these rules as a guide: (1) start with the dull, drab colors before experimenting with bright shades; (2) the darker the day or night, the darker the lure should be; (3) the smaller the eel, the brighter it may be.

Since all baitfish including eels have

The Cow Killer is a plastic monster nearly two feet long.

The size of the eel that you select depends on three things: the limitations of your tackle, the size of the fish you're after, and the size of the bait the fish are feeding on. You control the first factor. The second and third can be learned only through careful observation coupled with a certain amount of educated guessing.

Trollers can use eels of any size that may be right for the fish present and the bait at hand. Casters, on the other hand, are sometimes limited by the weight their rods can handle. When fish appear to be hitting a variety of different lures, it is often wise to stick to the old rule of "the bigger the lure, the bigger the fish." But when a specific type or size of bait is being taken by the fish, use an eel of similar size and appearance.

The right color can make a big difference. Eels in nature are basically dark on the back and light-colored on the under-

the ability to alter color or intensity of shading to some degree, a lure that can do this is universally acceptable. We have found that the clear plastic eel with a tint of brown stain will blend with most colors of a submarine environment and appear quite natural. An eel of this type appears almost sand-colored when worked along a sandy beach, but seems to darken immediately when the sand gives way to rocks or grass.

We call this color "chameleon" and if I had only one color of eel to fish with, it would be this clear, slightly-tinted type that matches almost any situation that an angler, or a striper, may encounter.

When fish are actively feeding on the surface, casting is probably the sportiest and most productive method, but when the fish are deep on a rip or scattered over a wide area, nothing beats trolling. For trolling eels in water 10 to 18 feet deep, monofilament line is best. Water deeper than 18 feet calls for lead-core or wire line, or mono or Dacron line fished from a down-rigger.

Monofilament lines can be run directly to the lure by means of a snap-connector, although some fishermen prefer a separate leader or at least a shock-leader tied to the end of the fishing line with a blood knot. My rule of the thumb for striper leaders is: let the leader be at least 50 percent heavier in test than the fishing line to be effective. Leaderless mono lines get more hits, but also lose more fish by being frayed or cut by a striper's scales and rough gill covers.

The snap connector that is attached to the eel head must have a well-rounded bend so the eel head may move freely in the connector. Anything that prolongs the effective "nose" of the action head will modify the prime action rate of the eel, usually for the worse.

As in casting, the first thing the troller must do is determine at what trolling speed his eels achieve prime action. This is usually a good bit slower than the speed for other successful striper lures. In some very swift tidal currents it is almost impossible to troll eels except at slack tide because of the need for high speed to keep the boat in position over prime bass locations during the run of the tide.

Make sure your eels are completely sub-merged and free of disturbance caused by the boat's stern wave when you test them and the boat for proper speed. Sometimes a small bubble of air will collect in the bend of the action head, and this will radically alter or destroy the action of the eel if it is not jerked clear of the action head.

Once the proper speed has been established, let out line until you feel the eel bouncing bottom. Then take in enough line to raise the eel somewhat above the bottom. Marking your lines for distance will give you an accurate estimate of how much line you must put out to troll the eel at a given depth. A sounding machine, of course, is a must for determining the depth of the water.

In eel-trolling, there is nothing wrong with putting your rod in a rod holder. Jigging the rod will only spoil the eel's prime action. But holding the rod in hand will allow you to feel your lure working every moment, and will let you know if you snag bottom or have the faint "tap" that often is the prelude to a heavy strike. You can also work the eel by slow-motion sweeps of the rod, imitating the kind of rising and diving action that the surf caster gives the eel on the retrieve.

Ordinary natural eels are difficult to troll in swift currents such as are found at Montauk, Cuttyhunk, Beavertail, Nantucket, Sandy Hook, and often at Cape

Clear plastic eels have the ability to take on the coloration of the water or bottom where they are fished, a quality possessed by some eels and fish.

Hatteras. But new, specially-designed trolling eels now make it possible to use these great striper-killers in fast water. It is quite important to "work" these with moderate sweeping rod action.

The caster's choice of plastic eel is often dictated by his preference in tackle. Light tackle spin fishermen or bait-casters use 3/8 to 3/4 ounce lures. Surf spinning anglers can usually handle lures of from 3/4 to 1 1/2 ounces. "Conventional" (revolving spool) casters use lures weighing from 1 1/2 to more than three ounces, and some supermen with Hatteras Heaver rods can use eels weighing as much as six ounces.

The great advantage that the caster (from boat or shore) has over the troller is that he has complete control over the prime or special action that must be applied to the eel. It is not always easy for the troller to vary his speed, but the caster can vary the speed of his retrieve at will and, because he must hold the rod, he gets constant feed-back from the lure and the fish via the fishing line.

The most important factor that the caster must bear in mind is the effect of waves and currents on the eel. Over these he has little control except to vary his retrieve speed and special rod actions to suit the situation. For example, casting up-tide will require a faster retrieve in order to maintain prime action than will casting down-tide. But as a lure comes down-tide and passes the caster, he must slow down his retrieve speed to keep the eel moving at prime action speed.

Sounds complicated, doesn't it? Solving these problems makes you a better fisherman, and puts more fish on your stringer.

In a strong current such as is often found in an inlet, the best strategy is often to cast out the eel and let the current alone provide prime action. You retrieve only when the eel is no longer in fishable water. When a strong surf produces a heavy undertow, you can sometimes take fish by casting short and dropping the eel back on free-spool through the undertow, then retrieving at high speed with the eel on the surface. Here you don't get the hits on top, but down deep, as the eel wobbles and dives, scraping the bottom with the undertow carrying it out against light finger pressure on the line. This is perhaps the trickiest of all eel maneuvers to pull off, but it's a killer when it works.

The final secret of using the plastic eel is knowing when to quit using it. Under some conditions, stripers definitely will hit other lures when they won't take eels. This is liable to be more true in daylight than at night. Plastic eels are wonderful lures, but they have their limitations. The wise angler always has a selection of proven jigs, metals, and plugs with him and when conditions dictate a change, or his intuition gives him a poke, he does not hesitate to change lures.

But at night, during morning and evening twilight, and on dark, overcast days a well-worked plastic eel is hard to beat. It fills a large gap in the practical striper angler's lure box, and it is well worth the time and effort required to master its many capabilities.

1 4 / Basic Knots

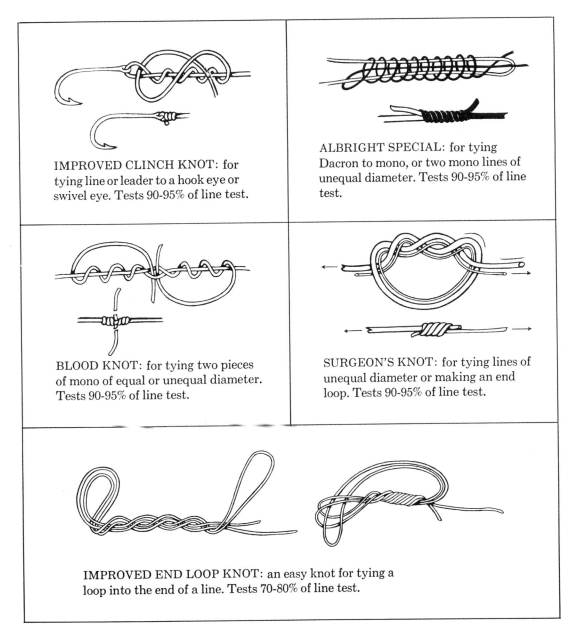

IMPROVED CLINCH KNOT: for tying line or leader to a hook eye or swivel eye. Tests 90-95% of line test.

ALBRIGHT SPECIAL: for tying Dacron to mono, or two mono lines of unequal diameter. Tests 90-95% of line test.

BLOOD KNOT: for tying two pieces of mono of equal or unequal diameter. Tests 90-95% of line test.

SURGEON'S KNOT: for tying lines of unequal diameter or making an end loop. Tests 90-95% of line test.

IMPROVED END LOOP KNOT: an easy knot for tying a loop into the end of a line. Tests 70-80% of line test.

Wire leader (haywire) twist
WHEN MAKING UP WIRE LEADERS TO HOOKS, swivels, or other important pieces of terminal tackle, always follow the three important steps shown here. Practice the wire leader terminal twist with spare wire and hooks until you can make smooth, even, non-rendering wire eyes with your eyes closed. Then when you have to re-rig in darkness, you won't have to light a light that might kill your night vision.

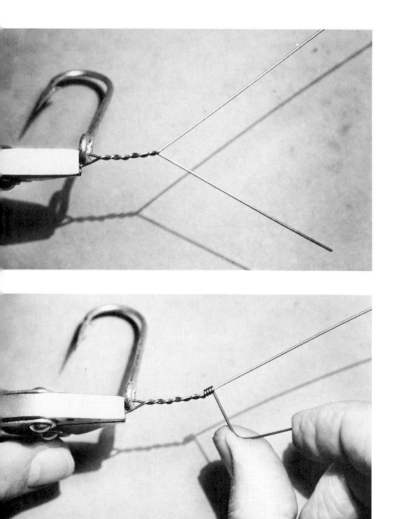

When making a loop in a wire leader on the eye of a hook, first bend the wire back sharply on itself, leaving a working end at least four inches long. Thread the wire on the hook eye, then grasp the end of the bent wire with pliers. Make at least six equal half-twists of the wire, marrying the two parts together.

After marrying the two parts of the wire in the manner of a twisted pair, make at least four close finishing turns of the tag end of the wire around the standing part. Then bend a right angle into the middle of the tag end as shown; the bent end should be parallel to the main part of the leader wire.

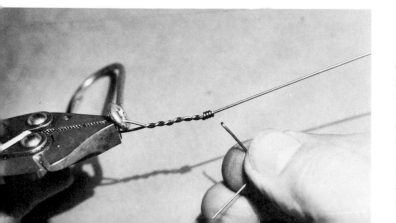

Grasp the wire end with thumb and forefinger exactly as in the photo above. By rotating the hand in a clockwise manner, twisting the tag end of wire sharply, you can break it off cleanly at the point where the last finishing turn leaves the main part of wire. The break should be clean, leaving no burr or point.

15 / Splicing and Marking Wire Lines

BEFORE YOU START TO PUT WIRE LINES ON your reels, consider carefully how you intend to use the wire. For example, will you be trolling deep in waters of from 10 to 30 or more feet in depth? If so, you may be wise to spool a full 100 yards of wire onto each reel. On the other hand, if you expect to work primarily in shallower water, seldom having to attain a lure depth of much more than 20 feet, 150 or 200 feet of wire may be quite sufficient.

Plan at the same time to mark your wire at various spots along its length so you can tell exactly how much wire you have out on any given rig when you want to.

Once you have decided how much wire you need on each reel and have a supply of wire at hand, find yourself an open ground area at least as long as the longest wires you plan to rig. If there is a wooden wall or fence at one end, fine. Drive a stout nail into the wall or fence, leaving the top inch of the nailhead exposed. Otherwise, pound a strong stake of 2×4 wood into the ground and drive the nail into the top of the stake in the same manner.

Carefully measure off on the ground the exact full length of wire that you need. Standing at the end of the measured distance away from the stake or nail, lead the backing line out through the guides of the rod and splice the end of the wire on the storage spool to the end of the backing line. The easiest splice for joining the wire to the backing goes as follows:

Tie a four- to six-inch loop in the end of the backing line, using the Surgeon's Knot. Next, using the end of the wire line,

tie a Becket Bend with the wire into the end of the backing loop, leaving a tag end of wire at least four inches long. Pull the Becket Bend of wire tight with your pliers, marry the tag end and the main part of the wire for a few twists, then finish off with close turns as you would finish off a leader eye. This splice will hold at least 80 percent of the original wire test, but may cut the backing after prolonged use.

To put the wire on the reel spool, run a dowel or screwdriver shaft through the wire line storage spool, lay the rod on the ground at the exact distance spot, then walk toward the nail-stake unspooling wire as you go. Let the wire storage spool rotate on its axle to prevent putting twists into the wire.

When you have the exact length of wire unspooled, cut it a few inches long, apply a stainless steel snap swivel to the end, and hang the snap swivel on the nail in the stake. Leave the wire stretched out on the ground and rig the other wire line rods with wire cut to exactly the same overall length.

Finally, starting at the stake end of the wires, measure off the various distances at which you want to mark the wires. Place a marker on the ground at each distance spot. I mark my 300-foot wires every 75 feet with marks at the 75-, 150-, and 225-foot locations between the stake and the rods. One of the easiest ways to mark wire is with spools of colored plastic striping tape. Get the narrowest you can find, about 1/8″ wide.

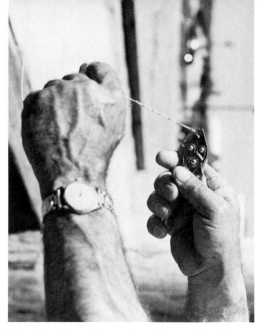

A measured shot of wire line is spooled on top of a reel one-half to two-thirds full of good quality soft-line backing.

The simplest wire-to-backing splice is to make a loop in the backing, then tie the wire into the loop using a Becket Bend.

Cut strips about six inches long from the various colors and wind the strips around the wires at the proper spot, marking each spot with the same color, naturally. A useful color code goes like this:

Black	—	75
Red	—	100
Green	—	125
Yellow	—	150
Blue	—	200
White	—	225

A strong, reliable splice is the so-called Basket Weave splice, illustrated in this chapter. The Basket Weave backing-to-wire splice is flexible enough to store easily on the reel, renders easily through roller or ring guides, and will hold 90 to 95 percent of the test of the wire or backing, whichever is the lighter.

A bad kink in a wire line should be repaired by cutting out the kink and splicing the two wire ends as illustrated. If you have to lengthen an existing wire, use this simple wire-to-wire splice. It will hold 80 to 90 percent of the original component test.

Lead-core wire lines are favored in some areas. They usually are color-coded on the outside nylon sheath. Tie a lead-core wire line directly to backing line with the Becket Bend, whipping the final bend with dental floss so it won't hang up in the rod guides.

Wire lines of any type that are used in salt water require special care after use. Wash the reel and line liberally in fresh, running water to remove salt. Stretch out each wire ashore and inspect it for kinks. Loose kinks can usually be un-bent with the fingers, but a tight kink must be cut out and the wire spliced at that spot.

If solid Monel wire starts to feel hard and stiff after considerable use, this is because the metal is starting to become fatigued. Eventually it will crystalize and fail when you need it badly. The cure is to remove old, stiff wire and replace it with fresh wire before sudden, unexpected wire breaks cost you fish and good tackle.

Backing line usually does not take much of a beating, but you should cut off the last few feet of backing each time you splice on fresh wire. Take care of your wires and they will give you many days of excellent fishing.

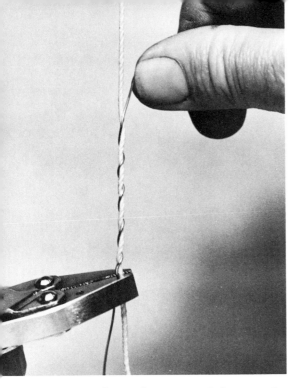

(1) To start the Basket Weave Splice, tie the end of the backing line to a firm object like a heavy desk, and tie the main part of the line to your belt buckle so you can lean back and put a strain on the line. Take the tag end of the wire, at least six inches long, grasp wire and line together, and wrap the wire tightly around the line, working away from you.

(3) Shift the pliers to the body of the turns and apply several close finishing turns.

Next, keeping strong tension on the (2) line by means of your pliers, wrap the wire back down over its own original turns, laying the turns on as strongly as possible. The wire should actually bite into the backing line and form a non-slip grip.

Cut the tag end of the wire off close (4) and bend the burr end in onto the main wire so it is smooth to the touch. The Basket Weave Splice is not easy to make, but will hold 95 percent of the wire's rating.

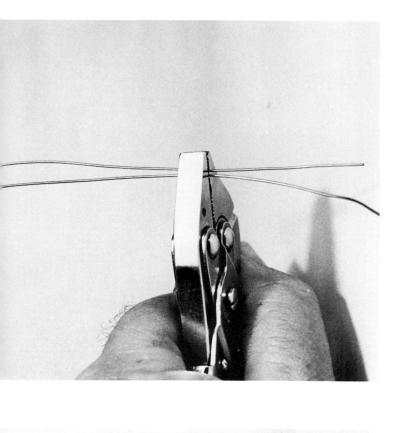

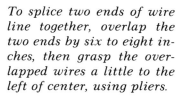

To splice two ends of wire line together, overlap the two ends by six to eight inches, then grasp the overlapped wires a little to the left of center, using pliers.

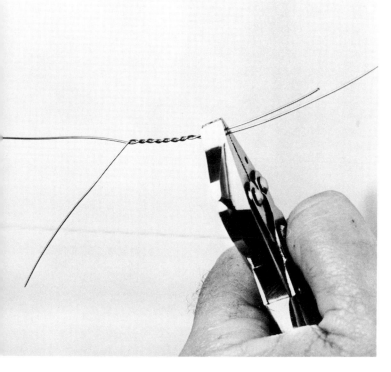

Holding the pliers firmly in the left hand, marry the two parts of wire together carefully, taking at least eight half-turns and forming a true, even twisted-pair.

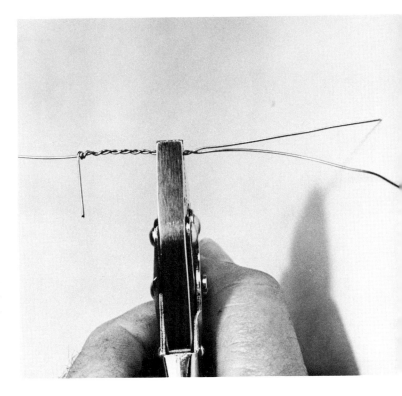

Finish off the twisted-pair by taking several close finishing turns with the tag end of the wire over the main part. Cut close in and bend down the end.

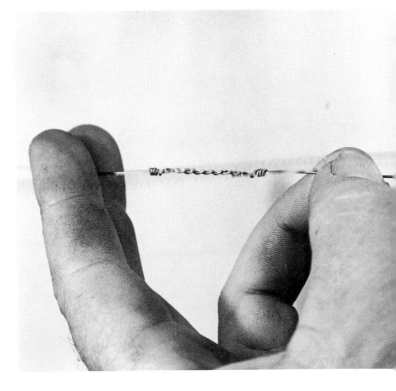

Finish off the other end of the splice the same way. The twisted-pair or "hay-wire" splice will hold up to 90 percent of the rated strength of the wire line.

16 / How to Read Flashing Sounders

FLASHING SOUNDERS OF THE PORTABLE TYPE are useful for finding fish and locating good bottom in daylight or darkness. Portable units like the Lowrence "Fish-Lo-K-Tor," illustrated, are reasonable in cost and use self-contained batteries.

Flashers display their information on a circular dial face marked in feet or fathoms. A neon bulb on a rotating arm makes one flash at the zero position and other flashes at positions indicating the depth of fish or the bottom. An educated eye quickly learns how to interpret the flashes in terms of fish and different kinds of bottom formations.

The following pages give specially prepared examples of displays found in areas where stripers abound. The sketches were used originally in *Sportfishing* Magazine and were prepared from the Lowrence operating manual.

Left: The easiest bottom to read with a flashing sounder is one composed of smooth gravel or hard, smooth clay or sand. A sharp, clear echo from hard bottom shows as a bright, narrow band at 20 feet. *Right:* When the boat moves from hard to soft bottom in the same depth, the mud absorbs some of the signal and the display flash is weaker and wider. Turning up "gain" will restore a bright signal.

Left: Here the boat moves left-to-right over projecting rocks. The lowest flash is hard bottom. Momentary flashes at various depths indicate tops of rocks. Fish sometimes simulate a rock display. *Right:* Continuing left-to-right, the boat passes over a submerged ledge. Rock projections register as bright bands lasting only while they are in the cone of sound. Flashers require constant watching.

Left. Fish swimming close to bottom often show like rocks, but the flashes from fish are usually not as strong as those from rocks and appear as fine lines or a red smear. *Right:* A school of fair-sized fish in midwater will show as a close series of fine lines or a dense, bright band of quick red flashes. The bottom line may lose some of its brightness and clarity.

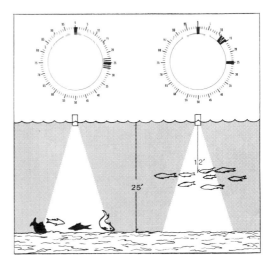

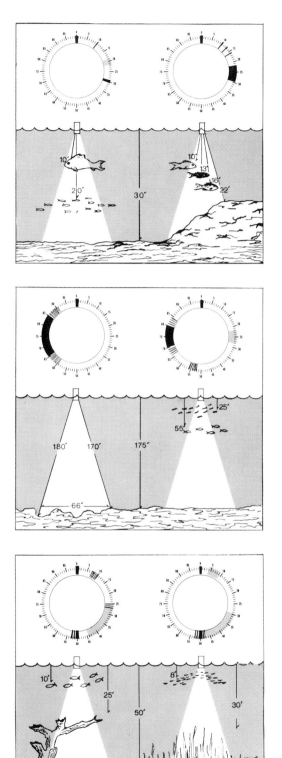

Left: You can often tell the size of fish by the flashes they make. A single large fish gives a bright, hard flash. A loose school produces a weak red shading or shifting lines and flashes of red. Right: Medium-sized fish at mixed depths show many thin red lines or flashes. The sloping bottom here is indicated by the broad, bright clear bottom band made by echos from varying depths.

Left: Many flashers can indicate depths greater than those on the dial. Here a sounder with 100 foot range indicates rough bottom at an average depth of 175 feet. Great depth causes the bottom flash to spread. Right: Smoother bottom at the same depth narrows the bottom band. Bait fish at 25 feet form a shaded band at that depth. Larger fish at 55 feet are indicated by shifting bright lines or flashes of red.

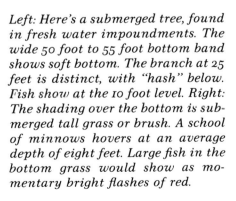

Left: Here's a submerged tree, found in fresh water impoundments. The wide 50 foot to 55 foot bottom band shows soft bottom. The branch at 25 feet is distinct, with "hash" below. Fish show at the 10 foot level. Right: The shading over the bottom is submerged tall grass or brush. A school of minnows hovers at an average depth of eight feet. Large fish in the bottom grass would show as momentary bright flashes of red.

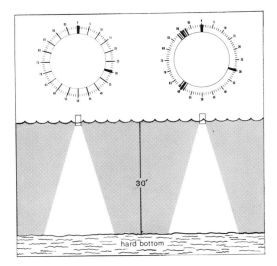

Left: There is always a reason for strange flasher displays. Here the boat is moving fast and air entrained under the hull makes the "picket fence" of sharp spikes. Solution, relocate the transducer. Right: Turning up the gain too high will cause the dial to register second and third bottom readings caused by the bouncing of the signals between the bottom and boat's hull. Solution, turn down the gain.

Left: Radio-frequency interference from faulty ignition causes evenly-spaced spikes that migrate around the dial. Solution, eliminate the ignition or electrical malfunction. Right: Portable sounders can be used to indicate depth and find fish through ice. Place the transducer in a depression full of anti-freeze, or suspend it through a fishing hole cut in the ice.

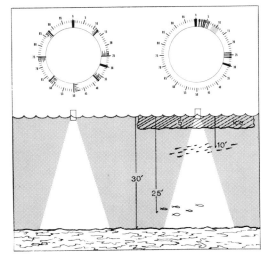

17 / Surf Fishing is Different

TRADITION HAS IT THAT THE FIRST SURF FISH-erman was an Indian brave, a member of Massasoit's tribe that succored the Pilgrims during their early winters on the cold New England coast. This brave's outstanding trait was laziness. He was so lazy, in fact, that the only gainful employment the tribal chiefs could get him to do was to sit on top of Plymouth Rock fishing with a rawhide line and a lobster tail lashed to a huge hook of bone and sinew.

He never caught any fish, but at least he was trying.

One night the Indian tied the line to his great toe, the better to stretch out under his blanket for some sleep. At the crack of dawn some of the Pilgrim Fathers were awakened by a loud yell and a heavy splash. Hauling on their breeches and jerkins, they hurried down to Plymouth Rock in time to see the Indian, swimming mightily, being dragged out to sea by a huge, unseen fish.

They launched a shallop, rescued the Indian, and hauled in a striped bass so big it took three of them to lift it into the boat. That night the grateful tribe gave the Pilgrims the first New England clambake, the main course of which was the great striper, baked whole over a slow fire. Since then New Englanders have been farthest out on the rocks when the striped bass are running.

Surf anglers await action on a beach of the North Carolina Outer Banks.

The earliest casting tackle was simplicity itself. Casting rods had not been invented, so fishermen wound hand-made horsehair or Sea Island cotton lines on wooden bobbins or circular hand-casting spools made from steer horn boiled to make the horn pliable. Lead was for important things like bullets, so sinkers were usually round stones held in a tiny net bag made of fine rawhide thongs. Hooks were hand-forged from wrought iron nails. Bait was any old fish offal, clam meat, or slightly dead lobster tails that might be handy.

Casting was something to watch, from a distance. The caster either faked his line down on the sand beach or coiled it carefully onto the circular casting spool, from which it would peel off very much like a modern spinning reel spool. Grasping the line five or six feet up from the sinker and hook, he began whirling the sinkers around his head in a great circle, gradually letting line out between his fingers to work up more momentum. Some casters needed a circle 25 or 30 feet in radius for casting.

When he was ready the fisherman let the line go, aiming it seaward. Once in a while the line would break from the tremendous centrifugal force and people for scores of yards up and down the beach would duck as a couple of pounds of stones went whistling overhead. Oddly, this primitive method caught fish.

Casting rods as we know them did not come into being until well into the nineteenth century after efficient metal reels

Art Passmore models the surf fisher-man's uniform: chest-high waders, web belt, and sun glasses.

Milt Rosko prefers oilskin pants worn over hip-high conventional boots for twilight beach fishing in mild weather.

had been perfected. The earliest surf rods were huge affairs of greenheart, hickory, or other hard, flexible wood. They were patterned after the older English salmon rods, but were longer and heavier. Sea Island cotton line was popular, but linen line was better.

The first quality casting line was a hand-laid linen material perfected by Captain Lester Crandall on the island of Cuttyhunk for the famous Cuttyhunk Fishing Club. First made in 1865, "Cuttyhunk line" was the standard of comparison for high quality fishing line until supplanted by modern synthetic lines in the mid-1950's.

Nowadays, braided Dacron line is the standard surf casting line with most revolving-spool ("conventional") reels, while monofilament is favored with spinning reels. Fiberglass has become the universal rod-building material, replacing hardwood, split bamboo, Tonkin and Calcutta cane, and laminated woods. Specific

recommendations for various classes of tackle for surf fishing are made in the chapter on "Tackle for Stripers," so let us continue this discussion in the vein of what makes a successful surf fisherman tick.

Of all the many forms of modern salt water sport fishing, surf fishing has the greatest appeal to the rugged individualist. People usually don't just suddenly decide they are going to take up surf fishing as a hobby. They have to grow into the sport through early exposure. For every hundred thus exposed, perhaps five ultimately stick it out to become full-fledged beach rats.

Some writers have called surf fishermen masochists, but this is misreading the character of the fishermen. They revile cold, dampness, hunger, and lack of sleep as bitterly as other mortals. But they are made of tougher fiber and willingly undergo physical torment and mental anguish, not because they secretly enjoy pain, but because they covet the sense of achievement that comes with success with the fish in the face of difficult conditions. The best of them represent a breed of sportsmen that is rapidly becoming extinct in this modern world.

Sociologists see this as a throwback to the early, bloody primeval hunter's urge. This may be so, but the surf fisherman sees it otherwise. To catch stripers you must be able to master discomfort and frustration without losing your powers of concentration, perception, and analysis. You must master yourself before you master the fish.

In the very old days, a surf fisherman's mobility was limited by how far he could walk. Nowadays, the modern four-wheel-drive recreational vehicle has given surf fishermen transportation that vastly increases their shoreside cruising range while at the same time provides the amenities of life in the form of a mobile place to sleep and prepare hot meals. The early beach buggies, however, were much simpler.

Early records and photos depict ancient trucks and autos used regularly for transportation on the North Carolina Outer Banks as early as 1915. The ubiquitous Model T Ford gave beach fishermen a cheap, rugged vehicle that would run on naphtha-and-kerosene when gasoline was not available. The idea of a motor vehicle equipped with big tires for running on soft sand spread rapidly to New Jersey, Long Island, and Cape Cod.

After World War II, the military Jeep's success on sand soon bred a new class of tough, powerful vehicles that could go almost anywhere. These proved just great for day fishermen, but surf anglers who wanted to spend more time on the beach away from home needed sleeping quarters on wheels, and a fantastic array of converted trucks and station wagons soon populated the more popular beach fishing rendezvous. The ultimate beach buggy now appears to be a four-wheel-drive pickup truck with camper body, quite often towing a beach-launchable outboard boat on a light trailer.

Outfits of this type made possible the Nova Scotia Striper Safaris of 1966 and 1968, described elsewhere in this book.

Besides a suitable beach buggy or other beach vehicle, what are the basic equipment requirements for successful surf fishing? The following is a representative list:

- Chest-high waterproof casting waders.
- Light and heavy waterproof parka jackets.
- Felt, chain, or spiked rock creepers.
- Military web belt for carrying equipment.
- Short-handled gaff on safety line.
- Fish-stringer line or light chain.
- Plug or lure box to wear on belt.
- Head or neck light for night fishing.
- Sheath knife.
- Fishing pliers in sheath.
- *Tide Tables* for the fishing area.
- Spare coil of leader material.
- Pocket hook hone.
- Light, medium, and heavy casting tackle.

Note carefully the item "*Tide Tables* for the fishing area." Few fishermen are more tide-conscious than surf fishermen. The best tide situation for fishing varies from place to place, and season to season, but each major fishing area has a definite seasonal tidal pattern that surf fishermen recognize and use in planning their trips.

At some places on Cape Cod, for example, many experienced surf men favor the period from half-ebb through low water to half-flood. Low water makes it possible to get further out on rocks that are submerged at high tide, and sometimes reveals details of offshore rock, reef, and bar formations that are not visible at high water.

But on Long Island, for another example, many anglers seem to prefer the period from two hours before high water to two hours after high water. The important point to recognize is that the fish are highly individualistic in the way they respond to tidal stimuli, and the *Tide Tables* can only serve as a guide in the light of expert local knowledge. Stripers are predictable in the broad sense, but, if one thing is true about their habits, it is the fact that you must expect the unexpected.

This is part of what makes them so attractive to fishermen of boat or surf persuasion. Another thing that makes them popular is the way stripers occasionally respond with great enthusiasm to a new design of plug or lure. In the days before mass production of lures, most surf fishermen cast their own lead and tin jigs and carved their own plugs.

In those days a fisherman could find many fish that had never seen an artificial lure. You might say that the fish were uneducated, that they hadn't yet been to school. When you happened onto a plug design that had superior fish-catching ability, you didn't have hundreds of other fishermen all fishing with duplicates of the same superior plug.

I remember vividly when the red-head popper first came into popularity back in the days right after World War II. This was one of the very first mass-produced plugs and surf men had a prejudice then against anything turned out by machinery. But those red-head poppers did something to the stripers that no other plug I had ever seen could do. They brought big, angry bass up in deep water to wallop and smash at the aggravating plugs as if the stripers' lives depended on eliminating the menace.

Charles R. Meyers' plug-caddy rides on his left hip. The short gaff is hung from a stout belt-hook and rubber lanyard.

For a short while it was heaven. You didn't have to study the tides or look for bait. A popper splashing out on the water seemed to bring stripers running from as far as they could hear the commotion the plug made as you popped it heavily with your Calcutta rod.

But one of the true mysteries of these fish is the way they seem to be able to communicate a state of danger to other fish in the school. Gradually, the red-head popper lost its magic appeal. By the time it had achieved general acceptance the fish were wise to what it did to them. Poppers are still great plugs, but they have never gone back to being as heroically deadly as when they were first invented.

Present-day surf fishermen really don't have to do much experimenting with home-designed plugs if they don't want to. You might almost say that most of the basic experimenting with plug design has already been done. Take, for example, the many good poppers, darters, swimmers, and deep-divers that are now available.

Sometimes making a choice among all the styles is not easy. Larry Green in another chapter has named his choice of ten best Pacific surf lures. The following is a similar and slightly larger selection of top Atlantic casting lures by Charles R. Meyer. Note the duplications.

- Creek Chub Jointed Pikie.
- Arbogast Dasher (with propeller).
- Mirro-Lure.
- Atom Striper Strike.
- Creek Chub Striper Strike.
- Gibbs Darter.
- Yellow-Silver Rebel.
- Alou Black Plastic Eel.

A surf fisherman's standard kit includes: Gaff on coiled-rubber lanyard, fish stringer chain, plug and jig caddy on web belt, rigged eels, plugs, metal jigs, lamp.

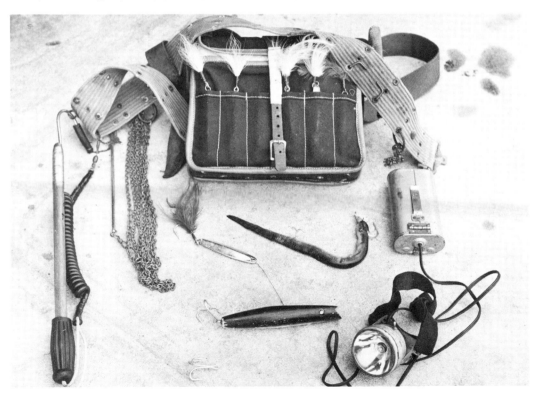

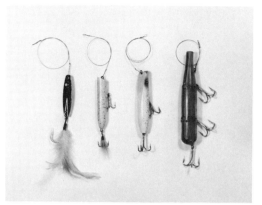

Four popular Eastern casting lures are the Louis Cilhar Chrome Block Tin Squid, the Atom Midget Popper, the Stan Gibbs Darter, and the Reverse Atom.

- Upperman Bucktail.
- Kramer Smiling Bill Bucktail.
- Diamond Jig.
- Louis Cilhar Block Tin Squid.
- Hopkins Hammered Finish Jig.
- Atlantic Auto-Cast.

The surf caster's basic lure kit consists of popping plugs for surface action, swimming plugs for sub-surface use, diving plugs for bottom-bumping (a technique borrowed from fresh water bass fishing), metal jigs for distance casting, weighted bucktails for bottom-scraping, and artificial eels for twilight and night fishing. Taking them in the order mentioned, here's how they should be worked.

Popping plugs. These are retrieved with short, rapid jerks of the rod tip to make them splash water from their concave or slanted forward ends to simulate an injured bait fish on the surface. Many of the new solid plastic poppers sink slowly at rest, but ride the surface and pop beautifully on retrieve.

Place a popper in the eddy down-tide of a big rock or out in the open tidal current up-tide of a bar rip where it will drift down into the rip face as you work it back inshore. Vary the popping rate and occasionally let the plug sink or drift quietly for a few seconds. When you get a hit, strike the hooks home the instant you feel line tension. Plugs with not more than two treble hooks are now honored by the IGFA if fished by casting, not trolling.

Blue-silver, blue-white, and white-black are good color combinations. When squid or whiting are a common local bait, light-colored plugs with touches of yellow and red are very effective. Popular weights are two to three ounces for most surf conventional and spinning tackle. Poppers are best in daylight hours.

Surface swimming plugs. As the afternoon sun descends, it pays to switch from poppers to swimmers, especially when diminishing wind and tide contribute to calmer water. This is when a sub-surface swimmer can be very deadly. Most swimmers have a metal lip or nose plate, the angle of which can be adjusted by bending to achieve a deeper or shallower swimming depth.

Instead of working the rod vigorously as with poppers, cast the plug out and start to reel in quite slowly. Many swimmers are designed to float at rest, reversing the system used with poppers. You should be able to feel the plug "wobbling" slowly against your rod tip. Sharp-feeling plug action means you are reeling too swiftly. Vary the reeling speed and let the plug come to surface rest several times during each retrieve.

Strike after a half-second of hesitation when you feel a bump or hit. Use a very moderate drag. If you miss hooking the fish, keep right on retrieving with longer and more frequent pauses. You may entice the fish back for a second try. Practice

Felt-soled creepers, worn over the boot-feet of waders, improve traction on slippery rocks and hard bottom when wading. Other wading creepers are armed with golf-type spikes or chain treads across soles.

with swimming plugs in daylight and clear water so you can see how they act under different surf and tidal conditions. Learn to recognize good action by feel alone, because when you're into fish you probably won't be able to watch the plug anyway and only your sense of touch can guide you for proper swimming action.

Deep diving plugs. These relatively new plugs are quite difficult to use in shallow water, especially over seaweed or rocky bottom, but they are great for getting down to very deep fish where deep water comes in close to the beach or rocks. Some deep-divers sink at rest and by experimentation you can sink them to a predetermined fishing depth before starting to retrieve by "counting down" the required number of seconds.

Others, like the Rapalas and Rebels, are quite light and achieve depth through the paravane action of their big metal diving lips. By varying the speed of your reel retrieve you can vary the depth. A slow retrieve gives a shallow run whereas a fast retrieve makes the plug dig deep. On sandy or mud bottom, it often pays to make the plug root along the bottom as you retrieve it.

Metal jigs. When there's a gale of wind blowing onshore or across your casting path, a metal jig may be the only lure that will cast far and accurately enough to reach the fish. The familiar old eastern keel jig, exemplified by the famous Cilhar and Tuma jigs from Montauk, cast like bullets, yet ride on the surface with a fast retrieve. At medium or slow retrieve they work much deeper.

The equally famous Hopkins family of hammered-finish jigs is widely used by surf men for fishing at the extreme limit of casting range, and in very dirty water caused by heavy surf and strong winds. The best rod action with any metal jig is a fairly constant retrieve speed combined with a moderately fast pulsing rise and fall of the rod tip. The action should not be as strong as when popping a popper, but stronger and more rapid than that used to swim a swimming plug.

Weighted bucktails. Under some wind and sea conditions, the weighted bucktail jig equals or outperforms a metal jig, especially when used with relatively light spinning tackle. Bucktails appear to be especially useful in early spring and late fall when smaller fish are running. They are primarily daytime lures and must be retrieved at high speed to achieve good action and avoid fouling the bottom.

Artificial eels. These very useful lures are thoroughly covered in the chapter on plastic eels by Al Reinfelder. Both artificial and natural eels are worked in exactly the same manner Slow and easy does it, with the best action at twilight and after dark.

The future of striped bass surf fishing

looks clouded. As more private beach-front owners and seaside towns put restrictions on recreational vehicle travel along their beaches, and as more people seek to use our beaches for other than fishing purposes, fishermen suffer loss of fishable beach territory. At the same time their ranks grow more numerous.

Many former surf fishermen now do a good part or all of their 'longshore fishing from boats. They say they have to in self defense. It is a fact that a boat-borne caster has ten times the mobility of his surf-bound brother. But strong year-classes of young stripers in the vital mid-Atlantic breeding range, and along the San Francisco river delta reaches, give promise of excellent fish stocks for a number of years to come on both coasts.

One thing is certain. There will always be strong-minded men and women who glory in overcoming personal and natural obstacles if the struggle leads to good fishing. To these people the call of the high surf is a wild call and a clear call, a call that cannot be denied. They are the ones to whom surf fishing is wonderfully different.

FRANK T. MOSS AND CHARLES R. MEYER

18 / Nova Scotia Striper Safari

ONE OF THE MEMORABLE MOMENTS OF ANY trip to a distant land is coming face-to-face with an old friend. This happened to me back in the late summer of 1965 when I was covering the International Tuna Cup Match at Wedgeport, Nova Scotia, but not in the manner one might imagine. The friend was not human, but my old fishing adversary—the striped bass. In a way it was almost an anticlimax.

I was on the press boat together with several other writers and photographers, waiting patiently for one of the contestant boats to hook a tuna in the lower reaches of the Tusket River, inside of famed Soldiers Rip. Fog lay around the islands, but the day was calm and mild. Over yonder a small flock of terns was wheeling and diving to the surface of the water.

As we drifted closer, I saw several fair-sized fish break under the birds. "Probably pollock," said a man from Boston.

Just then a fish that looked as if it would go a good five pounds broke the water completely and in the half-second that it was exposed I got the shock of a lifetime. "Hey!" I finally managed to blurt out, "That was no pollock. That was a striped bass!"

"You're imagining things," said the Bostonian. "This is too far north for stripers."

Then the boat's captain chimed in with, "What in thunder is a striped bass?"

The rest laughed and I felt foolish, but back at the Grand Hotel at Yarmouth I met a local salmon expert who admitted to hooking an occasional striper while trolling big streamer flies for salmon in the Chebogue and Tusket Rivers. Then a friend of his told about a man he knew up at Annapolis Royal on the eastern shore of the Bay of Fundy who caught "several dozen every summer" on rod and reel.

Back in the fleshpots of New York, the idea that an undiscovered, possibly extensive population of stripers might exist in Nova Scotia kept bubbling away on the back burner of my mind. I met a writer who actually had caught stripers in Canada, but his experience had been in New Brunswick, across the Bay of Fundy from Nova Scotia.

"No reason why there shouldn't be plenty of bass in Nova Scotia," he opined, "but the Canadians don't like 'em. They call 'em 'Yankee bass' when they catch them in their herring nets and they sell them for fertilizer."

The idea of anyone selling stripers for fertilizer sounded odd to me then, but further investigation proved it to be occasionally true. Then it began to dawn on me that if there were stripers enough up there to be a sometime problem to the herring fishermen, there might be enough around to afford some damn fine light tackle fishing, Yankee-style. Here was the germ of a really great fishing story. Were Nova Scotia waters hiding a species of fish that, someday, might be as valuable to sportsmen as their vaunted salmon?

My problem was that I'd probably never be able to afford the time to find out, personally. But as editor of the then new magazine *Sportfishing,* I did enjoy a certain amount of leverage among fishing clubs, outdoor writers, and those who untie the purse-strings of resort territories like Canada and Nova Scotia. I saw a way to explore vicariously the suspected striped bass potential of Nova Scotia and extract an exciting fishing story for my magazine in the process.

The result was that the following summer an assault team of seven truck-campers, each trailing a small outboard boat, and 15 men, headed toward Nova Scotia sponsored jointly by *Sportfishing* Magazine, the Long Island (N.Y.) Beach Buggy Association, and the Nova Scotia provincial government.

Expedition leader was Charles R. "Chuck" Meyer, then a field editor for the magazine. His crew was made up of specially selected volunteers from several Long Island beach buggy and striped bass associations. Their avowed purpose was to explore as much of the southern Nova Scotia tidewater area as they could in four short weeks and tag and release as many stripers as they could. While tagging of stripers had been carried out in Canadian waters previously to a limited extent, no U.S. returns of Canadian-tagged stripers had ever been recorded.

Our ultimate hope was that this very modest tagging effort might establish definite clues to a suspected interchange between Canadian and mid-Atlantic U.S. striper stocks. How this hope was eventually fulfilled is the climax of this story, but first let us learn in Chuck's own words how he and his doughty striper-hunters did it:

We arrived late in July with the blessing of the Nova Scotia government, but without a hint as to the whereabouts of any striped bass. We had four weeks to explore a coastline longer than that of New York, New Jersey, and Connecticut combined. In all this vast coast there was not one local striper expert that anyone could point out.

Our initial near-catastrophe happened

A front hitch on a Jeep camper truck makes launching a big outboard boat easier in a Nova Scotia river during the joint U.S.-Canadian striper safari.

at Annapolis Causeway near the Bay of Fundy town of Annapolis Royal. We were preparing to recover skiffs from the water before moving farther on. Jimmy Wilbert had warned me, "Leave your big Jeep truck on high ground so we can use the front power winch to haul out anyone who gets stuck in the mud."

"Good idea," I agreed—and promptly forgot!

Rain began and, in a hurry to retrieve our 16 foot Boston Whaler and its trailer, I backed the 7,000 pound Jeep camper-truck down the dirt bank. Zook! The rear wheels broke through the shallow surface hard pan, miring the truck to the axles in mud. It was low tide, and the Fundy tide can rise 60 feet in five hours.

Ronny Keith and Jim Wilbert took over the Jeep, letting me work the big electric winch up front. Jim hooked the cable to a solid-looking tree ashore while Ronny put the Jeep into four-wheel drive and low-low gear. Like a wounded buffalo the Jeep lurched up out of the soft stuff onto hard ground as the tide rose under the trailer wheels. Here was Lesson Number One of Nova Scotia amphibious fishing:

Probe the depth of the hardpan with a crowbar before you back down an untested bank, and make sure there is a stout tree or rock handy for your power winch.

It was here at Annapolis Causeway that we hit the first good striper fishing. Here we were fortunate to meet Cecil Atkinson, one of the few Nova Scotians who regularly and successfully fishes for striped bass. He is reputed to take as many as 1,000 school fish a season.

Cecil jumped when he first saw striped bass boil after our popping and swimming casting plugs. He was a bait fisherman, catching his stripers on bits of herring. Top-water plug action on light tackle was something new to him, and he loved it. In a couple of days he had taught us a lot about which phase of the tide to fish. With his help we caught and released a number of school fish, all with *Sportfishing* tags in them. But all too soon we had to move on.

It was in the tidal rivers of southern

Sometimes launching was more difficult. Here Yanks and Canadians muscle a light outboard skiff over a rocky beach somewhere in southern Nova Scotia.

Nova Scotia that we finally hit a stride in catching stripers. This is low, rolling country with salt and brackish rivers and sounds reaching far inland. Here our trailer boats came into their own and we did relatively little shore fishing. Jerry Dominy fell in love with a little inflatable Avon rubber boat with a flea-power 3.9 horse-power Evinrude motor.

All of our trucks had CB radio outfits so we could spread out and still keep in touch. Two portable sounding machines, a Lowrance Fish-Lo-K-Tor and a Raytheon DE-720B, proved to be extremely helpful. With them we were able to locate underwater bars, channels, rocks, and other prime striper pastures, and even schools of herring bait and stripers swimming too deep to be noticed from the surface.

Our Jeep truck with its Franklin camper body provided all the comforts of home including a hot shower and a refrigerator for perishable food and bait. Some of the other beach buggies, especially the homemade ones, found life a little more rugged. No one had any trouble buying food, fuel, or essential supplies.

Any truck-camper or mobile home working this area should carry two hydraulic jacks and pieces of heavy scrap lumber for jack bases. The tool kit should include a heavy lug wrench, sockets, road flares, a mechanical or electric air pump for tire inflation, puncture repair kit, shovel, electric fuses, lanterns, bulbs, hack saw, and either a ¼-inch breast drill or one of those wonderful rechargable portable electric drills.

One of the great charms of Nova Scotia is the friendliness and hospitality of the people. Ask for directions and you probably will acquire a temporary guide. Show the local fishermen how to catch stripers

A double-header hooked from shore along the rocky coast of the Bay of Fundy.

on top-water tackle and every door in town is open to you.

You have to bring your own tackle, though. Heavy import duties make U.S. tackle prohibitively expensive, and there just isn't any such thing as Canadian striper tackle. Oddly enough, experimentation showed us that we could catch stripers quite easily on ordinary fresh water bass rods, reels, line, and lures.

The facts we uncovered in our first Nova Scotia Striper Safari can be summed up this way:

1. There is a large, active population of school stripers along the Bay of Fundy shore from Annapolis Causeway south to the Chebogue and Tusket Rivers. The fish are there from May through October and follow much the same pattern that they hew to in the States. In late July and August we were actually fishing in the summer "slow season."

2. Most of the fish we encountered were schoolies under 15 pounds. We tagged and released more than 200, placing *Sportfishing* loop tags through the back skin behind the second dorsal fin.

3. We noticed that many fish carried a broken stripe, almost as if the side had been wounded, but without visible scar tissue. Biologists may some day establish these broken-stripe fish as a northern sub-race.

4. At Clarke Head, near Paarsboro, Gunard Bergman of our party and I talked with an old fisherman who showed us a picture of what looked like a 40 pound striper, taken years before. We caught no really big fish, but that does not mean that trophy-size stripers don't exist in Nova Scotia waters.

5. Local striper fishing is limited almost exclusively to fishing with herring bait, or trolling with big salmon flies and heavy salmon fly-casting rods. We found the fish highly responsive to U.S. casting and trolling tackle, and often took fish where natives swore they could not be present.

Yankee tackle takes Bluenose striper in the sluiceway at Annapolis Royal.

But they had to catch a few themselves with our tackle to believe that it wasn't some sort of trick fishing. There are few local bass fishermen and almost no guides. Visiting Yanks have to find their own fish. But this is no real problem for experienced striper anglers.

6. If you felt like trying Nova Scotia for stripers as we did, what should you do to get ready? First, be sure to enlist the aid and companionship of at least one more dependable truck-camper rig and friendly, experienced fishing buddies. Next, provide all the normal things you'll need for a several-week vacation in the boondocks, plus the following list of essential tackle:

• Light and heavy casting rods for each man.
• Plenty of spare line, leader material, etc.
• A good supply of your favorite casting plugs.
• Hooks for making up bait-fishing rigs.
• A good light open boat and trailer.
• CB radios in cars, plus walkie-talkies.

Yankee tackle takes Bluenose striper in the sluiceway at Annapolis Royal.

• Salt water fly tackle if this is your dish.
• Waders, boots, foul weather clothing.

You'll need a fresh water fishing license for angling in inland areas, and if you have CB in your rig you'll need a Canadian reciprocal license. You can get information on obtaining these important items, as well as travel routes and ferry schedules from Maine and New Brunswick to Nova Scotia by writing to: Nova Scotia Travel Bureau, Department of Trade and Industry, Halifax, N.S., Canada.

When Chuck Meyer and his angling explorers got back to Yankeeland, their enthusiasm for Nova Scotia striper fishing sparked many East Coast U.S. fishermen to try their luck in 1967. Some hit good fishing, others did not do well. Generally, those who planned well got fish.

In 1968, a second fishing-tagging expedition was mounted, this time under the sponsorship of *Sportfishing* Magazine together with the Canadian government and the provinces of Nova Scotia, New Brunswick, and Prince Edward Island. Most of the fishing was confined to New Brunswick waters, where upward of 200 stripers were tagged.

In retrospect, perhaps the most exciting event of the entire Nova Scotia Striper Safari affair took place quietly in New York in mid-March of 1967. A letter arrived from a commercial fisherman located at Indian River, Delaware. It contained *Sportfishing* tag No. 00551 which had been affixed to a small striper in the Chebogue River, N.S., on Sept. 4, 1966, by Hugh Cook, a Nova Scotian who had helped our lads from Long Island, and with whom tagging equipment had been left.

Here at last was direct proof of at least

some interchange of stripers between Canada and the mid-Atlantic region of the U.S.A.

As time went on, more tags were returned by cooperating U.S. and Canadian sport and commercial fishermen. Early in 1971 *Sportfishing* did a cursory analysis of the tagging effort that had been made in 1966 and 1968, and discovered that a total of 36 tags had been returned at that time.

Six of these came from U.S. waters, five from Nova Scotia, and one from New Brunswick. They were recovered from a wide coastal area between Rhode Island and Chesapeake Bay. Numerous recoveries of fish tagged in Nova Scotia and New Brunswick suggested strong permanent or over-wintering stocks in the Canadian provinces. But the really exciting news was the first discovery of the migration of fish from Nova Scotia to Delaware Bay.

A tiny sampling such as this should not be interpreted as positive proof of a massive striper migration, but it does show what intelligent sportsmen, using modern tools of science and their own fishing skill, can do to unearth important biological and environmental facts. Now it is up to Canadian biologists to prove or disprove the suspected existence of breeding stripers in the waters of New Brunswick and Nova Scotia.

And to think that it all began with the chance observation of a single bait-chasing striper on the Chebogue River, that warm September day back in 1965!

Art Passmore applies a Sportfishing *tag to a small striper taken in Nova Scotia.*

Bob Zwirz wades ashore with a brace of bass caught with fresh water tackle in the upper reaches of a North Carolina coastal estuary.

19 / Stripers Invade Fresh Water

THE TELEPHONE IN THE ARKANSAS GAME AND Fish Department office at Little Rock jangled and one of the men picked up the receiver. "I want to report catching a strange fish," a masculine voice stated.

"What kind of fish?" the fisheries technician asked.

"I dunno. It's got seven dark stripes down each side of its back and it looks like a white bass, but it's ten times bigger than any white bass I ever saw."

"Where did you catch it?"

"I speared it skin diving in Lake Ouachita."

"We'd like to see that fish," the state man said. "Could you bring it to the laboratory?"

"Well, I'll have to borrow a pickup truck. You see, it weighs 55 pounds."

The state biologist shouted. "Fifty-five pounds! Man, it sounds like you've just caught a new state record striped bass!" Then a sudden thought struck him. "But you've also broken the state game law. Only scaled, non-game fish may be speared in Lake Ouachita!"

There was silence on the phone, followed by a deep sigh. "Forget I called. I'll take it home and hold a fish-fry." The connection went dead with a click.

"Damn!" exploded the biologist. His agitation was understandable. Lake Ouachita had been stocked with striped bass in the late 1950's and had produced at least one 35-pounder. Here was what might have been proof that fish of that early stocking had survived and grown to record size in the new environment.

This true story was reported recently by the Arkansas Game and Fish Department. It highlights the exciting fact that all over the United States a new and splendid species of salt water game fish is becoming available to fresh water fishermen, a species that may soon produce many land-locked specimens in the 50 to 60 pound class.

How did the great fresh water invasion of striped bass get started? Where can fresh water stripers be caught now? What is the outlook for the future? The answers to these questions began with a great biological experiment that started quite accidentally back during World War II.

When the waters of the Santee River in South Carolina were impounded on November, 1941, to create the 170,000-acre Santee-Cooper Reservoir, no one thought that damming the river might create a land-locked population of striped bass. During the 1940's occasional catches of stripers were made by sport fishermen interested primarily in bream and largemouth bass.

By 1955, creel census reports showed that stripers were becoming an important part of the sport fishing catch in Lake Marion and Lake Moultrie, the twin lakes of the Santee-Cooper system. Then, in 1959, the fish reached a peak of abundance and made up 40 percent of the total catch of all species taken from the lakes.

According to Robert C. Stevens, then Assistant Unit Leader of the North Carolina Cooperative Fishery Unit at Raleigh, N.C., this tremendous catch reflected both an exploding striper population and a decided preference of the local fishermen for striped bass.

Until 1959 there had been widespread opinion that spawning adult bass had to return to salt water between breeding seasons. But the great land-locked striper explosion in Santee-Cooper could have resulted only from extensive successful natural breeding in rivers tributary to the artificial lakes. Careful investigation soon proved this to be a fact.

At first it was thought that the Santee-Cooper population was unique in its ability to breed in fresh water, but breeding populations of stripers appeared in Kerr Reservoir on the North Carolina-Virginia border and in Millerton Lake, California. This indicated that if the special spawning requirements were present, these fish would reproduce themselves in fresh water elsewhere.

Evidence was found in 1968 and in subsequent years that striped bass introduced into the Colorado River from California had reproduced successfully. Fishing for stripers is now becoming a popular sport in the Lake Havasu region of Arizona.

Biologists early recognized the striped bass as a potentially tremendous fish for hatchery management and introduction into new salt and fresh water habitats if problems of obtaining fertile eggs and raising the delicate fry could be solved. But their first efforts were not very successful.

At first the biologists tried to capture ripe females, strip them of their eggs, and fertilize the eggs with milt from live, captive males. This proved easier to plan than to carry out. Many females were captured alive, but discouragingly few batches of fertile eggs resulted. The problem soon was recognized as being primarily how to determine when a given female was entering her critical 60-minute post-ovulation period when the eggs could be stripped from her and fertilized.

Hormones were tried in 1962 and 1963 at the Moncks Corner, S.C., laboratory to try to induce females to ovulate in captivity, but few viable fry resulted. While females with immature eggs could be induced to ovulate, no fertile hatch would result. It was foreseen that, to be effective, hormones would have to be applied to the females at a critical period in time prior to the onset of natural ovulation.

The problem of how to forecast the time of ovulation in any given female striper was solved when a catheter-sampling technique was worked out. Eggs drawn from the female with a catheter were compared to photos of eggs of known age before ovulation. By simple comparison a forecast for the fish in question could be made.

From then on little difficulty was experienced in obtaining fully ripe eggs from gravid females and in fertilizing them with milt from captive males. This technical break-through has made possible the rearing of millions of striped bass fry under laboratory conditions.

From 1964 through 1968, nearly 500-million striped bass fry were produced at the Moncks Corner lab alone. The vast majority were introduced into waters and reservoirs in South Carolina other than Santee-Cooper. The remainder were distributed to many state, federal, and a few foreign agencies for stocking and rearing.

The year 1968 was an outstanding one in terms of success in hatching, rearing, and stocking of striped bass fry in fresh water. Twenty-nine different agencies including South Africa and the Soviet Union received viable fry from the three major hatcheries at Moncks Corner, S.C., Weldon, N.C., and Brookneal, Va. More than 150-million fry were produced.

As catch data began to filter back from waters where stripers had been stocked, it soon became apparent that introducing small striper fry into waters with estab-

These fine stripers came from under Jim Woodruff Dam in northern Florida. Dixie stripers tend to be mainly fresh water fish.

lished predators was, to a large extent, fruitless. Big black bass, pickerel, pike, trout, and even sunfish and catfish ate up the helpless fry like candy. But stocking with larger fingerlings certainly was more successful.

Not only are fingerling stripers less vulnerable to predation and to mortality during transport, their tolerance of temperature extremes and pH quality of water is greater. Optimum conditions for young fry, Bob Stevens states, are 65° F. and 8.0 pH.

As more was learned about the condi-tions under which stripers thrive best in fresh water, more and more state agen-cies began to clamor for fingerlings to stock in their big lakes and reservoirs. A happy fact of striper life is that shad and alewives are prime fodder for raising big, strong stripers. Hundreds of inland im-poundments and lakes have superabun-dant shad and alewives and precious little else in the way of fish.

The dynamics of establishing a new population of predatory fish in a body of water also became known. In Santee-Cooper, for example, stripers exploded in

Fresh water stripers respond to the same fishing methods used in salt water.

population until 1959, when the number of stripers present became too great for the food and space available to them. A massive die-off removed the excess population, and since then striped bass in those lakes have lived in healthy togetherness with the native species of game and food fish.

Where can you find fresh water stripers and how can you catch them?

Santee-Cooper is still considered the finest and most productive fresh water striper locality, but a number of other bodies of water are coming rapidly to the fore. Kerr Reservoir, mentioned earlier, and its associated Gaston Reservoir in northern North Carolina provide some spectacular fishing.

Bill Cochran, writing in *The Carolina Sportsman,* tells of a 29 pound 12 ounce brute captured from a boat in the Roanoke River by Walter E. Echols who had to thrust his hand in the fish's gills to land it because it was too big to fit in his landing net. Two other anglers fishing from the bank under Kerr Dam landed 16 stripers totaling 273 pounds. Their stringer of

fish was so heavy they could not lift it from the water!

The Kerr Reservoir population has been producing since 1960 and is claimed to be the second major fresh water impoundment to start producing landlocked stripers by strictly natural breeding. Each April and May the fish are found in the Dan and Roanoke Rivers above Kerr Dam, spawning. Here the eggs have the moving water they require for the first 72 hours of their incubation before they hatch.

But Kerr Reservoir fishermen will have to go some to top the mighty 55-pounder caught in Santee-Cooper in 1963 by Tiny Lund. Judging by the growth charts now available, Lund's record striper was probably about 20 years old when caught, which might make it one of the very early stripers to have been bred in the closed Santee-Cooper system.

Several reports tell of a 63-pounder said to have been taken in Georgia waters, but no particulars are available as to who caught the fish, where it was caught, and what method was used.

In 1967, one-million striped bass fry were stocked into Lake Navarro Mills and Lake Bardwell in Texas as the start of that state's five-year striper stocking plan. Several million fry and fingerlings will have been stocked in these and other Texas lakes by the time the program has been completed.

Kansas introduced the fish into Cheney, Wilson, John Redmond, and Elk City Reservoirs at about the same time. In the fall of 1968, schools of juvenile stripers were observed below Davis Dam on the Colorado River near Bullhead City, Arizona. In subsequent years the Colorado River and Lake Havasu have produced stripers that have gone between 15 and 20 pounds.

The St. Johns River in northern Florida seems to be the southern limit for stripers along the Atlantic shore. Good striper fishing is to be had among the black bass near Welaka. Hot bass fishing is also experienced under Jim Woodruff Dam. In 1969 an airlift of young stripers from North Carolina to Choctawhatchee Bay in northwestern Florida was aimed at establishing a new population of stripers in the rivers tributary to this northwestern Florida bay.

As biologist James M. Barkuloo has pointed out, in its southernmost range from Georgia across the northern arc of the Gulf of Mexico to the Mississippi delta, the striper is primarily a fresh water species, rarely entering salt water.

Catching them in fresh water does not vary much from the systems used to catch them in the ocean. The fresh water fisherman does have one tremendous advantage over his salt water brethren. In fresh water the striper responds to the 24-hour cycle of sunlight and darkness as does any respectable bass, and no special hocus-pocus has to be called upon to figure out the effect of tides on fresh water stripers.

Tackle should be of the best quality. Remember that the rapid growth of striped bass fingerlings puts them into the four-to-five pound class within two years of stocking, and up to ten pounds within four years. In lakes where stripers have been in residence for ten years, 30-pound fish are a definite possibility.

Good quality bait-casting tackle, spinning tackle capable of handling smallmouth bass or pike up to 15 pounds, and fly rods of salmon caliber are adequate for most fresh water stripers. Fill the bait-casting reel with 20 or 25 pound test line, or spool monofilament line of at least 15 pound test onto your heavy-duty spinning reel. Fly leader tippets should test at least eight or ten pounds.

My personal favorite outfit for live bait fishing or casting for stripers on both salt and fresh water is a nine-foot, two-piece Shakespeare Model SS535 fiberglass rod. On this, for casting, I use a medium sized salt water spinning reel filled with 15 or 18 pound test mono. For trolling and live bait fishing, I switch to a good level-wind, star drag reel filled with 20 pound test mono.

As a companion outfit in the fly fishing division, I like the new Pflueger Supreme nine-foot salt water fly rod rated for WF10 or WF11 line. Matching this rod is the Pflueger Supreme No. 578 salt water slip-drag fly reel. Such an outfit gives me an excellent chance of hanging onto any big striper that I may encounter on either fresh water or salt.

Salt water anglers know that big stripers like big baits, especially if the baits are of the herring family. Live shad, herring, or alewives make the finest kind of big-striper bait. Lacking such bait, you'll find that minnows, large shiners, baby perch, small suckers, waterdogs, crayfish, and eels are excellent striper killers.

At Kerr Dam, Woodruff Dam, Santee-Cooper, or Lake Havasu, where mixed small-to-medium stripers are found, most anglers use spinning tackle for casting from shore or bait-casting equipment such as they would use for big black bass, walleyes, and the like for casting or bait fishing from boats.

Stripers, especially the big ones, make powerful runs and seek underwater obstructions when hooked. A strong, smooth-working reel drag is a must. Supply yourself with a really good long-handled dip net and a strong gaff on waters where gaffs are allowed.

Like their cousins the white bass, stripers like to school together and chase bait fish at the surface. If gulls or terns are present, their hovering or diving over a particular spot on the lake is a sure sign of bait activity beneath. This is where you can practice the exciting system of "jump fishing" as it is called in Santee-Cooper and the TVA lakes.

When a school of bass starts to break the surface, feeding on bait, anglers in fast boats run up quickly to within casting range, then stop their boats and fire their casting jigs and plugs into the boiling fish. Almost every cast is a strike while the fish are up.

On some southeastern lakes a clever adjunct to jump fishing has been developed. Anglers who are in on the trick supply themselves with a few cans of cheap fish-flavored catfood before starting out. When a jump of feeding bass is found, they chum the area with the catfood mixed into a thin soup with lake water.

There is enough smell and taste in the chum to keep the bait and the bass up, looking for more, but not enough to satisfy their appetites. In a few areas such chumming is now illegal, so check your local fish and game laws before trying the catfood trick.

The best lures for casting, trolling, or jigging for fresh water stripers are the same ones that work well for largemouth bass present in the same water. Many proven salt water lures and plugs also work well in fresh water, but for the biggest stripers the lure supreme is live bait.

What is the future of stripers in fresh water? The great striped bass invasion has probably only just begun. Michigan in 1970 received more than 100,000 striped bass fry with which to begin experimental plantings in carefully controlled waters. Michigan biologists want to learn more about stripers before they loose these predators in the Great Lakes.

An extremely interesting development is now under way. Biologists hope to develop a fertile cross between the striped bass and its smaller cousins, the white and yellow bass. If a hybrid fish could be bred that would combine the size and other desirable qualities of the striper with the lake-breeding ability of its lesser cousins, inland sportsmen would have a new, valuable type of game.

Surely, such a man-made fish would revolutionize fresh water lake fish management. The future of striped bass in fresh water promises to be an exciting one.

Al Pearce with a school bass taken in Lake Havasu, a striper hot-spot of the landlocked Colorado River population.

20 / Beach Buggy Parade

EVER SEE AN ELEPHANT BOGGED IN DEEP mud? A three-quarter-ton pickup truck, piggybacking a camper coach, was down to the axles in the soft sand of Shagwong Beach, northwest of Montauk Light, on the eastern tip of Long Island. The 750 × 16 wheels spun futilely, the driver cursed, and the truck's clutch smelled like a boardinghouse frying pan. Only 200 yards ahead, a flock of gulls was working over a breaking school of stripers, hard in on the beach.

Zoom! That was an International Scout rocketing past, its four-wheel-drive whining like a banshee.

Ka-voom! That was a Jeep Wagoneer wallowing down the sand track like a ship in a beam sea.

Pocketa-pocketa. That was an unbelievable Model A floating across the treacherous sand toward the action.

Our friend in the truck remained mired until the blitz was over, stuck like a lamppost in solid concrete. When the fishing was finished, the others came back and dug him out. Disgusted and fishless he jockeyed his home on wheels back to the overnight camping area.

When you ride a heavyweight pickup camper, you do not venture on soft sand with fully inflated tires, somebody finally told the driver. Neither do you cramp your steering wheel hard over, nor do you floorboard the accelerator suddenly if you want to keep from getting stuck. If you intend to explore the ocean shorefront in search of stripers, there are tricks to the trade beyond sticking a surf rod in a bumper holder and tromping on the gas pedal. Here's a capsule version of the fundamentals, collected by angler-drivers from Cape Cod to Fire Island and the Jersey shore.

Can an ordinary car be used successfully along the surf line? No, at least not without specialized equipment and a great deal of sand-driving skill. Ordinary highway vehicles are too low-slung to negotiate the heavy ruts. A few station wagons, panel trucks, and carryalls are suitable to conversion, but you're better off starting with a vehicle designed for off-highway work.

For uncomplicated, fast transportation to and from surf angling hotspots, nothing beats a compact four-wheel-drive. You can't carry excess cargo in a Universal Jeep, or in an International Scout, but you're not trying to haul 4,000 pounds of rolling home over the sand, either. With oversize wheels and tires 820 × 15 or larger, deflated to 13 to 15 pounds of air, you can scuttle around on soft sand without difficulty.

Many surf men prefer to camp out in a converted panel truck or walk-in delivery van. Here, imagination is the secret to utilization of space. Two-wheel-drive vehicles traverse soft sand quite well when fitted with oversize lock-rim wheels and big, low-pressure "baldie" tires.

Ultimately, you can employ a big coach camper on a husky pickup chassis, but you'll need the biggest lock-rim wheels you can get. I advise 900-size six-ply tires capable of absorbing considerable flex from under-inflation. Remember, use low inflation only on the sand. *Never* run at highway speeds without reinflating the tires to proper highway pressure.

Always carry two spares, a shovel, a good hydraulic jack, and a tube repair kit. Ocean sands often contain driftwood with big, hidden nails and spikes. CB radio in the truck or beach buggy, plus a walkie-talkie unit to take on the beach or out in the small boat, is now practically must equipment. Without radio you never know what the other surf rats are doing until the action is all over.

The best way to get started in beach buggy fishing? Join one of the many beach buggy associations along the coast. If you can't locate one in your area, write to United Mobile Sportsfishermen (UMS), care of George Chesley, P.O. Box 74, For-estville, Conn. 06010. George will be happy to give you the name of the beach buggy group in your area.

Beach buggy fishermen do a great deal more than just cruise the sands looking for fish. Their associations provide safety patrols for crowded public beaches in summer. They provide manpower and vehicles for such enterprises as the Nova Scotia Striper Safari, described elsewhere in this book. They cooperate with programs of beach conservation, fish tagging, and erosion prevention.

Most important, they preserve an independent, highly satisfying way of fishing, a way that harks back to older and less artificial days. Constantly they remind us that it is the quality of the fishing, not the number of fish killed, that really counts.

An antique walk-in van is typical of home-converted beach buggies.

This handsome converted panel truck has an auxiliary sleeping compartment on the roof.

The four-wheel-drive Jeep Wagoneer stationwagon provides excellent day-fishing off-the-road transportation. It carries a small outboard skiff on a cartop carrier.

A Boston Whaler is launched at a public ramp on eastern Long Island, N.Y.

A compact cooking unit folds into a box on the side of this home converted buggy.

A twelve-volt power winch is a handy emergency unit adaptable to most vehicles.

*A self-contained camper truck and trailable outboard boat gives the serious
'longshore fisherman range and mobility on land and water not enjoyed by
other anglers.*

2 1 / Fishing Pacific Stripers

STRIPERS WERE INTRODUCED INTO PACIFIC waters in the region of San Francisco Bay a few years before the turn of the present century. It did not take them many years to become firmly established and soon were important market and game fish. In the 1930's striped bass were made strictly game fish in California, not to be bought or sold on the market. At the time of this writing, the bag limit is three fish per day by sport anglers only, and each fish must be at least 16 inches in length.

While I have never fished for stripers in Atlantic waters, from what I read about eastern bass there is a lot in common between Atlantic and Pacific stripers—but with certain important differences. The most important point to recognize about Pacific stripers is their migratory and breeding cycle. Understanding how this cycle works is the basis of successful striper fishing in California and western waters.

From June to about the end of September, stripers of the central California population spend most of their time in coastal ocean waters outside the Golden Gate, fattening on such active bait as smelts, anchovies, and herring. This is the annual weight-gaining period and also a period of sporadic surf fishing activity, mainly on the 25 miles of beaches south of the Golden Gate.

The action is hot and heavy when the bass appear off California beaches.

When the fish start to enter the brackish water of San Francisco Bay in October, their feeding habits change. Quickly they turn to a diet of bottom worms, crabs, shrimp, and other slow-moving bay life. This is when they store up fat that will sustain them during the spawning runs in spring up the San Joaquin and Sacramento Rivers of the bay river delta region. The migration into fresh water for spawning begins in late February and early March and lasts through April.

During the up-river move, the fish largely stop feeding, although they will strike at a trolled or cast lure and at certain baits, much in the manner of river-run salmon or steelhead. This non-feeding of spawning fish in coastal rivers is one of nature's clever adaptations to promote the survival of a normally voracious species. If mature salmon, steelhead, or stripers were to continue to feed in rivers at the rate that they feed outside, they would quickly strip the rivers of food. The hatchlings would starve before they could make it to salt water.

After spawning is complete, the spent adult stripers come back down to the bay in May. They are ravenous, and by the end of June have stripped the bay temporarily of everything edible. This is when they start moving out through the Golden Gate to their summer ocean feeding grounds, completing the year's cycle.

You can see from this that the stripers of central California give sport fishermen three entirely different types and times of fishing action during a year. I have fished for these wonderful fish for at least 25 years and while my batting average is now a good deal higher than it was when I was younger, I readily admit that the striper is a fish with a mind of its own. My wife, Mary, tells me that it is good for my soul when I score an occasional goose-egg with the bass. Humility, she says, may make me cross, but it keeps me from being boastful. But enough of that. Let's get down to the brass tacks of Pacific striper fishing, beginning with one of my favorite methods, trolling.

San Francisco Bay is a natural for small boat trolling, and when the hungry stripers return to the bay in the spring after their spawning venture up the rivers, this great bay, plus its tributary waters of Suisun, San Pablo, and Richardson Bays, boat fishermen have a ball. This is when anglers using plugs, spoons, fly rod equipment, and bait find the fish most cooperative. But later on, when the fish are more scattered, trolling is the best way to find and catch them.

One favorite trolling rig is a heavy wire spreader that carries two small jigs on short leaders of different lengths. Two or three such rigs, trolled in a zig-zag or expanding-spiral search pattern over known striper territory usually will pinpoint the fish if any are present. The spreader looks a lot like an enlarged turkey wishbone. The two legs of the spreader are separated at an angle of about 90° and are 10 to 12 inches long. A snap swivel is attached to the eye or loop at the center, and a heavy mono leader of 15 to 24 inches is attached to each leg end.

Snap swivels at the ends of the leaders permit quick lure changing. Lures that work well are small lead-head jigs, rubber tubing lures, small feathers, small spoons, and small plugs. A combination I find very good is a small plug on the longer leader and a smaller jig on the short leader. This creates the impression that an immature game fish is pursuing a bait fish. Stripers are very competitive about food, and often seem to go out of their way to slam a plug-jig combination like this, apparently "thinking" that they are robbing that other little "fish" of his dinner.

Sometimes I replace the plug with a spoon. I find that spoons and metal jigs are more effective when dressed with a trolling feather or strip of pork rind dyed yellow. In shallow water no additional weight is needed with the two-lure trolling rig, but in deep water, especially where the tidal current is strong, it pays to snap a trolling sinker into the eye of the spreader.

Many anglers are now fishing with very light tackle and single lures. I've fished a great deal both ways, and have discovered interesting facts worth passing on about the most popular classes of trolling lures, spoons, jigs, and plugs.

Spoons. Chrome spoons that produce a slow side-to-side wobbling effect are deadly trolling lures for striped bass. Usually the hook is concealed with a spray of feathers lashed to the hook shank. Yellow or white feathers are the best. To add even more attractiveness, many anglers slip a narrow strip of pork rind onto the hook. Again, white or yellow pork rind is best.

If you are getting a lot of hits but few solid takes with this combination, you may assume the bass are striking short. Switch to tail-hook pork rind, or attach a tail hook to the main hook so it will get the short-biters.

You may find that you have to vary the size or length of the spoon to get results. It is always very important to match the size of your lure to the size of the bait fish the stripers are feeding on.

Gold, copper, or brass-plated spoons do not seem to be as effective as chrome-plated or white-painted spoons. I carry a small can of gloss white, quick-drying lacquer and often find that a quick spray job on older spoons will restore their attractiveness to the fish.

Different models of spoons often perform best at different trolling speeds. When trolling spoons, always select spoons that perform best at the same speed. If you troll one "fast" spoon and one "slow" spoon, it's almost impossible to arrive at a speed at which both spoons will troll equally well. This cuts your strike potential by as much as 50 percent.

Jigs. If you are using a weighted (lead-head) bugeye jig on line of 12 pound test or less, you'll seldom need additional weight on the line to achieve proper trolling depths. The jig itself will be heavy enough. My system calls for stocking my tackle box with only a few types of jigs, but several different *weights* of each type. I've always found it better to switch to a heavier jig than to add trolling sinkers to get a light jig down to the level at which the fish are schooling.

Hair or bucktail jigs generally seem to outproduce feather jigs in the San Francisco Bay area. Again, white and yellow are the top colors. Pork rind is just great on the hooks of bucktail jigs. You can buy ready-cut pork rind, or you can trim your own from big commercial strips. Don't cut the strips any longer than the jigs they are to be used on.

Most jigs are manufactured with the hook point riding up. This means that you can actually drag or bounce the jig over a soft muddy or sandy bottom without hanging it into the bottom. If you find that "bottom scratching" works well, don't forget that you have to pull in every so often to clean seaweed or other dirt from the hooks.

A secret-weapon mud-scratcher lure that works very well on ultra light tackle (six pound test and lower) can be made up as follows:

Get some big "Keel Fly" (offset shank)

The San Francisco Bay delta region is the primary breeding ground for West Coast stripers and also one of the major fishing areas for Pacific striped bass.

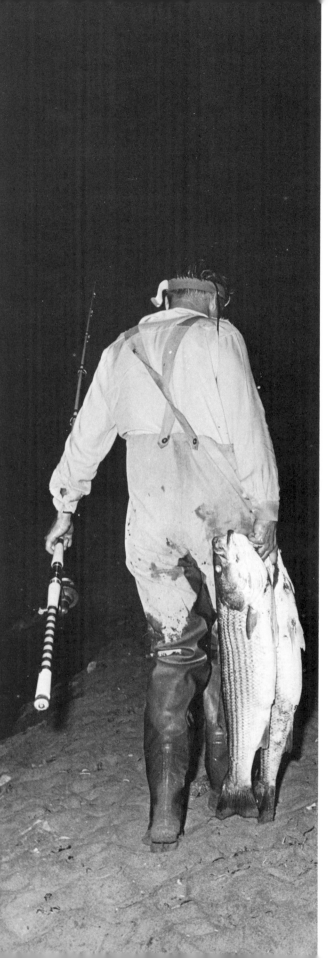

hooks of 6/0 size or larger. Wrap thin solid-core lead soldering wire around the shank of the hook to add weight. Then dress the shank with yellow wool and Mylar, and tie in a big "wing" and "tail" of stiff, yellow bucktail. Tie the "wing" so it projects back over the hook point, acting as a weed-guard for the hook. Drift over mud or sand bottom, gentling jigging the weighted fly over the bottom as you drift. It drives the stripers crazy, and you'll catch fish when other trollers and bait fishermen are getting ready to take the gas pipe for inaction.

Trolling plugs. While there are thousands of plugs on the market today, only a few have proven their ability to take stripers consistently in western waters. We have found that regular 5/8-ounce fresh water bass plugs seem to get more hits than larger plugs designed specifically for stripers. Maybe this is because we usually troll plugs for school fish rather than for big super-stripers.

Again, the colors white and yellow seem to get the most hits. Perhaps the most popular single plug for western striper trolling is a red-head with a white body. Either solid or jointed plugs will do, although I find that solid plugs seem to produce better action than jointed or two-piece plugs.

I prefer plugs with treble rather than single or double hooks and equip all of my plugs with sturdy nickel-plated salt water treble hooks of appropriate size. The "Flatfish" type of perch-like plug in recent years has played an important part in western striper trolling. I attribute this to the fact that our shallower bays and sloughs are infested with a small, flat, fish

Night fishing for stripers in California is relatively new, but is producing good catches for those who are properly equipped and have learned how to cope with the need to fish by feel in darkness.

called shiner perch, prime fodder for hungry stripers.

The new flap-tail and propeller-equipped surface plugs and the long, slender diving plugs are quite popular. Before buying a supply of trolling plugs, which may represent quite a few dollars of investment, it's a good idea to check at the tackle stores and among practicing striper fishermen to find out what plugs are really taking the fish. Here, again, it's my practice to stock only a few plug models, but several sizes of each important model.

What about trolling speed? I do not believe there is any "perfect" striper trolling speed. There are just too many variables and different circumstances to be considered. I try to troll at whatever speed produces the best action for my lures. Sometimes this may be fast, sometimes slow. As a rule, I find a fast troll as effective on stripers as a slow one. The important point is not the actual speed, but the fact that you are using lures matched to the speed, or making speed that gives good lure action.

When you are "bottom scraping" with jigs or other lures that deliberately dig the bottom, you have to go slowly for the lures to work. This may call for speeds of one to two miles per hour. But I have often been passed by big boats trolling at five or six m.p.h., and when we returned to the dock they had as many fish as we, although caught on different lures.

Perhaps the best all-around striper trolling speed is three to four miles per hour, or equal to a fast walk. In windy weather you have to watch speed carefully. Wind behind your boat may speed up the troll by two or three m.p.h., while wind on the nose may make a small boat stand almost still in the water.

But much as I enjoy trolling, I really get my biggest kicks out of surf casting for stripers. My favorite month is September. As I indicated earlier, most of the bass

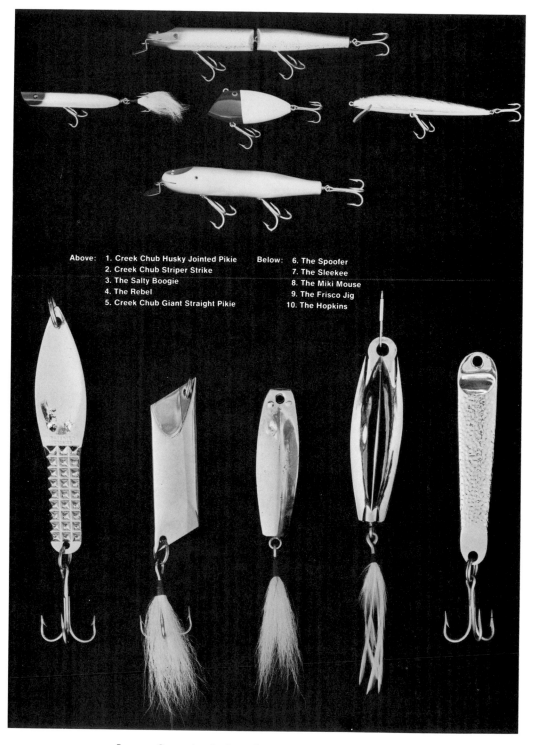

Above: 1. Creek Chub Husky Jointed Pikie
        2. Creek Chub Striper Strike
        3. The Salty Boogie
        4. The Rebel
        5. Creek Chub Giant Straight Pikie

Below: 6. The Spoofer
        7. The Sleekee
        8. The Miki Mouse
        9. The Frisco Jig
        10. The Hopkins

Larry Green's choice of ten top western striped bass casting lures.

that breed in the San Francisco Bay delta area vacate the bay for ocean waters during the summer. But summer is a time of vacation tourist crowds on the ocean beaches during spells of good weather, and cold fogs and chilly northwest winds for about two-thirds of the time. September is different with moderate surf, less fog, and bigger fish.

California surf fishermen use two distinct types of lures, plugs, and metal jigs. By plugs I mean lures that are shaped from wood or plastic to resemble various types of bait fish. Metal jigs are cast from lead, tin, or combinations of soft metals and are usually chrome plated. From the hundreds of lures that have been developed for the brisk surf fishing market, I have carefully chosen ten—five plugs and five metals—that are the real old reliables as far as California surf fishing is concerned. Let's take a sharp look at what I call the "Big Ten of the Western Surf" and see how each of these fine lures works.

First, we'll start with plugs. A fish-catching plug has to have good action at any speed of retrieve. Unlike the troller, who has constant control over his plug's speed, the caster has the factors of wind, current, swell, and undertow working either for or against him. His plug must be equally effective when reeled in at slowest possible speed, or hauled in against the uncontrollable thrust of a three- or four-knot current. It must also have good floating and top-water qualities, whether it's designed to work on the surface or down deep on the retrieve. The top water ability will enable the angler to work the plug over and around submerged rocks where the big stripers lie. All five of the plugs I have chosen have these characteristics to a superior degree.

The Creek Chub Striper Strike. This is a favorite plug among fishermen who fish a lot along rocky areas. When bass are "resting" among the rocks, this plug is used to wake them up. It is retrieved with short, sharp, jigging rod action that sends the plug chugging and splashing across the surface like a herring with a broken nose. Although it is not a large plug, it has weight and casts well.

The plug is equipped with two sturdy treble hooks, the after one of which is dressed with bucktail. It comes in an assortment of colors, but I prefer the darker combinations. To work it properly, you need a fairly light spinning or "conventional" casting rod with stiff action. The best line is between 12 and 18 pound test, although this is by no means absolute.

The Creek Chub Giant Straight Pikie. This big plug has proven itself as a real big-fish attractor, especially in the hot-pants color combination of yellow with big blotches of pink. Some anglers spray-paint their own. The plug, when new, is covered with a pearlescent finish that seems to be extremely effective in dark waters or at night. Night fishing in California for stripers was legalized a few years ago, and some of us are still learning new tricks for taking these great fish after dark.

The plug has an adjustable lip that permits the angler to retrieve it at almost any desired, reasonable depth. It also has good floating properties. The action is side-to-side, with little variation of action caused by changes of reeling speed. It is rather light for its size, and offers some wind-resistance to distance casting. Therefore it appears to be best used around rocks or ledges that are not at extreme casting range.

The plug comes with three sturdy treble hooks, but you can remove the first or second hook in case you wish to fish "strictly IGFA." Best rod is a fairly long stick with medium-light action. Line of up to 30 pound test may be used.

The Creek Chub Husky Jointed Pikie. Lest I be accused of being a paid agent for the Creek Chub people, let me remind readers that in California we do not have the great number of specialized striped bass plug manufacturers that East Coast anglers enjoy. I recommend the Creek Chub plugs because they catch fish. If somebody from Cuttyhunk or Montauk wants to send me some samples of eastern plugs, I'll be happy to give them a good honest test.

The Jointed Pikie is a monster of a plug, but it works like crazy when the very biggest stripers are around. The smaller fish don't seem to bother with it much, so if big fish are your aim, this is one plug that helps you to fish selectively. The mid-body joint seems to give the plug an especially tantalizing wiggle-action.

Because of its size and weight it is good for distance casting with Big Bertha tackle, although I prefer to cast metal into an onshore gale. I prefer a color combination with dark head and back and use it where there are rocks and deep holes well offshore, working it very slowly on the retrieve. The rod should be long, with medium to heavy action, and the line should be 20 to 30 pound test for very big fish.

The Rebel. Actually, the Rebel represents a whole family of slim plugs that very closely resemble certain types of live bait. I prefer the color combination that most resembles the mature anchovy. Anchovies are stripers' most popular ocean food. Any plug or lure that imitates the anchovy will catch many stripers in Pacific waters.

When retrieved at regular speed it has very good side-to-side action. It is light, so it cannot be cast as far as some other plugs, but it floats well and sometimes a very slow retrieve will take fish where a fast retrieve with the plug running under the surface only gets "bumps." It is wonderful when stripers are actively feeding on fair-sized surface bait.

The Rebel comes with a pair of sturdy treble hooks and has a fixed diving plate at the nose. Work it fast and it dives deep;

work it slow and it stays on top—great combinations of action in any striper plug. Very often it pays to vary your retrieve speed radically several times during each retrieve. This plug seems to work best when given frequent changes of pace.

Your rod should be light, with light action. The line can be any weight from 15 to 25 pound test.

The Salty Boogie. This unusual plug is completely different from any of the other four mentioned. There is one place, however, where it outshines the others. This is when the bass decide to give up anchovies on the surface and dive down deep to feed on surf perch. With its wide, heavy, deep body, the Salty Boogie does resemble a surf perch.

When retrieved fast near the bottom (this plug sinks when retrieved) the nose of the plug skims the sand and the body wriggles frantically in a very perch-like manner. The Salty Boogie has proved to be about the only plug or lure, not counting live bait, that will take stripers consistently when they are on a surf perch feeding binge. Few California bass experts will be caught without one.

Metal lures are fished mainly where distance casting is a major factor. Heavy and with relatively little wind resistance, metal jigs have greater casting range than most plugs. They are also used a great deal when bass are breaking and feeding actively in surface bait. This is when a fast cast, a quick retrieve, and equally quick unhooking of hooked fish are important. Later, when the bass hug the bottom after feeding, probing the depths with heavy metal jigs often gets hits where other methods fail.

The following are the five metals that I have found most effective in Pacific striper waters:

The Miki Mouse. This lure is one of the largest sellers on the West Coast. It does not have the high polish of some other

Larry Green gaffs a San Francisco Bay striper for Frank Guiggan. The boat is typical of West Coast outboard fishing skiffs.

metals, but it is extremely effective. Its large single hook is trimmed with bucktail. It comes in several weights with either a plain or dressed hook.

The Miki Mouse has a pitching, rolling kind of action and is a good school bass killer. It works best near the bottom. The best rod is a fairly light, stiff-action stick and the line should match the lure weight, starting with 12-pound line for the lightest models and going up to perhaps 25 pound line for the heaviest models.

The Sleekee. This lure reached the Pacific Coast only a few years ago, but it has proved to be a real killer. Its design and weight give it excellent distance without much casting effort. Action is spasmodic, dipping, darting, unlike any other casting metal. It drives stripers frantic.

The single treble hook is usually dressed with bucktail, which helps its attractiveness in dark or murky water. Here again you'll need a fairly light, stiff-action stick with line matched to the lure

153

weight. A normal retrieve speed without much jigging appears to be the best rod action.

The Hopkins Lure. For years, we westerners wondered what special magic East Coast fishermen found in the highly touted Hopkins hammered-finish flat-body casting jigs. Then some brave soul ordered a dozen and the rush was on. Few metals have proved so universally effective on stripers on eastern, western, or even inland waters.

The highly polished, hammered finish seems to imitate many types of scaled bait fish. Its weight and streamlined body make it a whizz to cast far in windy weather. The side-to-side action does not change materially at any speed of retrieve. It works best in rough surf, white water, and when the stripers are feeding on small- to medium-sized, swift bait.

The best rod, for distance casting, is a medium-light stick with medium-stiff action. The line should be a little on the heavy side, for the Hopkins attracts big fish as well as school stripers. Work the rod with a quick, pulsating, up-and-down motion to give the lure that wounded-bait look.

The Spoofer Lure. This flat, heavy lure is great for distance casting. Retrieved at normal speed, it rides with strong wobbling action just under the surface, its plated sides reflecting sunlight. I find my best action comes when I let the lure sink deep after casting, then bring it in by alternating fast and slow retrieves that vary the depth of the lure.

Retrieved at fast speed it splashes on the surface and sometimes you have two or three stripers chasing it, competing for a chance to grab it. When this happens, a radical change of retrieve speed, followed by quick reeling, will usually get you a strike. The same rod and line recommendations apply for it as for the Hopkins.

The Frisco Jig. This western-sounding jig actually originated on the East Coast, but it's red-hot on Pacific stripers. A well-made, highly polished lure, it has excellent light-reflecting ability and casts like a bullet. The single hook is trimmed with feathers. I sometimes substitute a hook dressed with bucktail, or a plain hook and a strip of pork rind.

The raised center and broad sides give the lure action that is effective at any retrieve speed. It is an excellent producer when worked in strong currents around rocks, a channel entrance, or over broken ledges. Surprisingly, it also gets hits from good sized stripers on sand beaches. In fact, one version of this jig was used for years at Montauk, N.Y., by anglers who preferred it over all others for sand beach work, or so my East Coast spy tells me.

The most productive surf fishing area in California is the 25 miles of ocean beach south of San Francisco. Surf equipment is identical with that used elsewhere, with one unusual exception. Quite a few surf casters have swung to using the single-action "sidewinder" Alvey reel, manufactured in Australia. The reel spool pivots on its frame so the line, in casting, spins off the reel the way it spins off a spinning reel spool. But the spool is cranked by a handle knob in the conventional manner after casting and after the spool has been rotated back into the normal retrieving position.

With the Alvey reel, it is possible to uncork tremendous casts, far beyond the distance of ordinary surf tackle. This is a distinct advantage when fishing shallow beaches where the surf breaks very far out and it is necessary to reach the breakers to hook fish.

The Alvey reel spool is connected directly to its knob handle and there are no gears or drag brake. You apply drag pressure by palming the spool rim with your hand. The Alvey reel may be old-fashioned, but it is very effective in the hands of a man who has mastered it.

Back in 1965, the California Department

of Fish and Game amended its regulations to permit night angling in the state's ocean waters. To those of us who had grown up knowing nothing but daylight angling for stripers, this opened a whole new world of adventure, and at times misadventure.

For example, we soon learned a cold, hard fact about Pacific stripers that we had never suspected. This was that while we could expect furious action during twilight and up to total darkness, the fishing action stopped at full dark as if the fish had slammed shut the barn door. For one thing, we couldn't see the fish in the dark and had no targets to which to cast. For another, we suspected that the same applied to the fish.

At first there was concern that the agitation to get night fishing in the surf had been for nothing. But a lot of good fishermen could not accept the fact that stripers could not be caught at night. A way would surely be found, and eventually it was.

Night fishing became an obsession with a lot of us and the rest of the fishing community began calling us "The Lamplighters," and thereby hangs an interesting tale. First, we had to learn all over again how to roam the rocks and beaches without getting hurt. Miners' headlamps soon became standard equipment, plus Coleman lamps for our base sites. But one development over all others led to eventual success with the fish.

We learned to fish slowly and easily, drawing each cast and retrieve out to last twice or three times as long as we did in daytime fishing. And we learned to use a special night-time attractant on our plugs and lures. It took a while, but experimentation proved that strips of *phosphorescent, light-sensitive tape* attached to our lures and plugs made them super-attractive to stripers at night.

Perhaps this is because Pacific waters hold a number of bait fish species that are phosphorescent after dark. In any event, night fishermen on the California coast now never go out without a roll of this tape and a good electric miner's lamp to shine on the taped lures and activate the tape.

We Californians have been fortunate. The striper is a tough, rugged, hard-fighting, good-eating fish. It has become thoroughly acclimated to Pacific waters through many generations of living here. It is legally protected and gives great fishing pleasure while providing much good food to hundreds of thousands of western sportsmen. But there is one big cloud on the horizon.

The ambitious water distribution plan that eventually will bring fresh water from northern California to dry southern California is bound to change radically the special qualities of the San Francisco Bay delta rivers where the fish breed. If the rivers are destroyed as bass breeding grounds, we may say goodbye to the striper as our top coastal game fish. That, after all these years, would be a true crime against nature and against the hopes and efforts of those early experimenters who brought these great fish from the East Coast.

Let's hope and pray it never happens.

RECORD SIZE STRIPERS ON THE WEST COAST? Nonsense! Any East Coast striped bass angler knows better than to believe that. Furthermore, the East Coast man will tell you that the Pacific Coast isn't capable of producing a striped bass larger than about 45 pounds, least of all in Oregon where the striper is a comparative latecomer.

Well, I guess East Coasters are entitled to believe what they believe, but for the sake of accuracy let's consider a few facts about Pacific coast stripers, facts not widely publicized.

It's true that the west doesn't have as big a striped bass population as is found in the east, but the fish have been here since the turn of the century and that's certainly long enough to become pretty well established. Until quite recently, however, there has been comparatively little angling pressure on them and this undoubtedly helps to account for the fact that few very large stripers have been reported or even landed in Pacific waters.

Nevertheless, super-size stripers have been hooked and some landed, although many have been lost due to the inexperience of anglers and inadequate tackle. California held the western record for some time with a 62-pounder caught from the Salinas River 'way back in 1937. A 63-pounder was taken in Isthmus Slough, Coos Bay, Oregon, according to Tom McAllister, outdoor editor for the *Oregon Journal*. This fish was also caught in 1937, but was never officially weighed or recorded.

Back in those days striper fishing in the Coos Bay region attracted a little attention, but not much. After all, this is primarily salmon and steelhead country. Big, tackle-busting striped bass were a curiosity that occasionally stripped some unlucky angler's reel, but which few serious fishermen bothered to fish for.

In recent years, however, big stripers have been taken with increasing frequency in the lower Umpqua and Smith Rivers near Reedsport, Oregon, approximately 27 miles north of Coos Bay. Through July and August every summer sturgeon anglers regularly pick up stripers ranging from around 30 pounds to better than 50 pounds on sand shrimp and various other sturgeon baits, and seldom make public mention of what goes on. Heck, any sturgeon fisherman worth his salt would rather catch sturgeon.

At the same time salmon anglers go out in droves from Winchester Bay at the mouth of the Umpqua River below Reedsport and ignore the stripers completely. When salmon are running, nothing else exists for a salmon fisherman. But in 1968, Mac McMannus of Salem, Oregon, decided to find out just how big some of these Oregon stripers were, and thereby hangs a mighty interesting fish talc.

Mac, an avid and persistant fisherman, had heard that tremendous stripers were present in the spring spawning runs of the Smith and Umpqua Rivers at Reedsport. This information came partly from a few local anglers and guides and partly from rumors that commercial shad net-

2 2 / Wanted—A Pacific Record Striper!

ters of the area sometimes netted stripers of what sounded much like world record proportions.

April 20, 1968, opening day of trout season for most Oregon anglers, found Mac in a party of four split between two boats trolling near the confluence of the two rivers. Deep-diving seven-inch Rebel plugs, trolled close to the bottom on the heaviest salmon tackle available, proved extremely effective. A total of six fish ranging from 24 pounds to 63½ pounds was boated that day. The 63½-pounder, which set a new Pacific Coast record, was actually quite a bit smaller than some of the fish the anglers hooked and lost.

Mac and his friends hadn't fished for an hour when they knew that their tackle was too light. They just couldn't keep the huge stripers out of the river pilings and broken-down piers along the shore with the 20 pound test line and medium rods that they were used to handling. McMannus swore that he hooked five fish that day, all plainly seen, that would have equalled or topped the 73 pound all-tackle world striper record caught by Charles Church at Quick's Hole, Mass., 'way back in 1913.

One fish, easily in the 70-pound class, promptly ran between pilings where a boat couldn't follow and sawed off the line on barnacles. The biggest fish of the day,

Don Striepke caught this 42-pounder at the Forest Pool of the Russian River.

157

Mac related, ran out approximately 150 yards of line. They chased it with the boat, regaining all but about 35 yards of line. By this time the fish had run into the shallows and was gouging around on the bottom. Its huge tail was clearly seen beating the surface before one final swipe parted the line. Going to the exact spot which was marked by a huge boil of mud, Mac put down an oar and measured the depth at five feet.

His 63½-pounder turned out to be 53 inches long, so there is a comparison to ponder. Would you believe 80 pounds? That's Mac's estimate!

The striper bass spawning season in Oregon generally lasts from March through June, although a late snow run-off causing cold river temperatures can delay this by a month or more in some seasons. If you are thinking in terms of a Pacific record striper, this is the time of the year to work at it.

During the spawning months, large female stripers come up from the lower river and the ocean. When they enter areas like the lower Smith River they group up, some anglers believe, in age classes. Clearly, when the huge females are concentrated like this in relatively small water, the chances of exciting, continuous action are good.

Best results to date have been obtained by trolling big plugs close to the bottom, although later in the season large spoon-head plastic eels, natural or blue in color, do quite well. Any plug resembling smelt or herring will get hits, but the Rebel deep-diver #2403 has been the most popular because of its built-in ability to go right to the bottom without added weight when trolled.

I use the new Sea Bee plugs by South Bend and find them to be very effective.

This Oregon boy caught his 60-pound striper in the Umpqua River.

Where deep water makes it necessary, I use a trolling sinker about six feet ahead of the plug. This gives me the added advantage of being able to feel the bottom with the sinker for snags. By raising the rod tip sharply and yanking strongly I can usually rip the sinker free of a snag and keep the hooks of the trailing plug from fouling the snag. Plug colors of blue, green, or silver seem to work equally well.

The big spawners are not actively feeding at this time and seldom have anything in their stomachs. They seem to strike only when the plug or lure is presented right down at the bottom where they prefer to lay. This is where paying strict attention to the tides has a great deal to do with success.

Because the fish are not actively feeding, it's not important to fish the run of the tide as it is in so many other areas. High and low water slacks are obviously the times when the boatman can control both boat and fishing gear most effectively. If the tides are not extreme, it is often possible to fish clear through a tide, but fishing the run of a tide, either ebb or flood, is never as successful as fishing slack water.

The tackle to use for a potential record fish is optional, but it had better be stout. A six- or seven-foot heavy salmon mooching or trolling boat rod would be a lot more practical than a light casting rod. Thirty to forty pound test monofilament or Dacron line should be the minimum, and the reel must have at least a 200-yard capacity together with a smooth, powerful drag. Remember those sunken snags and abandoned dock pilings! That's where most of the break-offs take place.

Remember also that International Game Fish Association rules allow you a leader up to 15 feet long for lines of 50 pound test and under. Don't be too proud to make that long leader out of mono or light wire testing 60 or even 80 pounds. It may make the difference between losing a trophy striper to the barnacles on a piling

or hauling in a fish that could put your name in the world record book.

Even with proper tackle, a large amount of luck is involved. Where snags and pilings are thick, troll with a very strong drag and heavy hooks on the assumption that if the fish doesn't tear himself off the hooks you may stand a better chance to keep him out of piling trouble. Provide yourself with a really stout gaff and if you do get a big striper up alongside, hammer that gaff into him as if you were driving home a 20-penny spike. Otherwise his armor-plated sides may turn the gaff point and you may lose a grand fish at the last instant.

The Umpqua Marina on Bolin Island, just north of Reedsport, is an excellent place to stay and a very good source of information. There's a good launching ramp and also boats and motors for rent. Overnight space for campers and trailers is inexpensive. Get yourself a map of the local area and have one of the local fishermen fill you in on the best spots to fish and when to be there.

During the late summer and early fall there is often red-hot fishing for mixed stripers of all sizes when the fish are schooled up and hungry after spawning, but before they migrate down the river. This is when surface plugs and big fly rod streamers take heavy toll of the beauties.

Bait anglers using herring, needlefish, smelt, or porgies often employ a sliding sinker on a long wire leader, or use the sinker on the line above a conventional leader swivel. This "fish-finder" rig is especially useful on snaggy bottom where deep-trolling is difficult or almost impossible because of hangups.

Why these big stripers have moved north from the San Francisco Bay area over the years and established themselves in certain rivers while apparently ignoring others is open to speculation. Perhaps as they moved north they explored a lot of rivers but liked only a few.

The many miles of estuarine water offered by the Umpqua and Smith Rivers apparently are made to order for big stripers. Head of tide water of the Umpqua is more than 20 miles from the ocean, and schools of stripers have been reported following runs of smelt clear up to Scottsburg, 20 miles above the Umpqua Marina. They were seen that far up the Umpqua recently in February, actively feeding on smelt and herring. These stripers had evidently not yet felt the spawning urge.

Local anglers, forgetting steelhead, rushed to the river with their heaviest tackle and reaped a brief but hectic harvest that included a number of stripers between 40 and 50 pounds. Most were taken by trolling, but a few fell to bank fishermen. A 12-year-old boy from Independence, Oregon, had his picture published in the local paper with a 60-pounder that he caught just below Scottsburg.

Where do the stripers go when they leave the river? Do they hide in the depths of the lower river and Winchester Bay, or do they go out to sea? No one knows for sure. Ocean surf fishing for stripers is unheard of in Oregon, although it is practiced widely further south in northern and central California.

It's quite evident that the experience, know-how, and finesse acquired over many years by East Coast striper experts has had little effect in Oregon. Perhaps a visit by some eastern striper experts at the right time of the year is what's needed to show western anglers how it's done.

But meanwhile, a handful of local enthusiasts really believe that they may set a new all-tackle striper record by the simple method of trolling a big plug down deep when the big females are schooled up in the rivers in spring and early summer. I'm convinced a new all-tackle record striper is swimming right now in Oregon waters. All it will take to catch the monster is some luck and an honest try!

This 62-pounder was taken in 1937 from the Salinas River.

2 3 / Secrets of a Hatteras Heaver

CLAUDE ROGERS AND I WERE LOOKING FOR fish in Chesapeake Bay a while ago when, without warning, a small, fast open fishing boat passed right over the school that we had just spotted. The fish sounded, naturally, but showed again perhaps 150 yards away.

"We can't get much closer without spooking them," said Rogers, a top distance caster. "Perhaps I can slip in another 30 yards."

I knew that the slap of our fiberglass hull against the Chesapeake chop would alarm the stripers. It was going to be a mighty long cast. Claude killed the engine when the fish were still at least 110 yards away. We were using stainless steel Hopkins jigs weighing 3¼ ounces and were using revolving-spool surf outfits, stiff sticks of the so-called Hatteras Heaver type that measured 10½ feet long. Our reel spools were filled with 30-pound test monofilament.

Claude cast first. When his jig splashed softly into the water he allowed it to settle before starting his retrieve. He had made only a couple of turns of the reel handle when his rod arched under the strike of a good fish. My cast fell 20 feet short of Claude's. I let the lure settle although I was sure the cast was a lost cause, but when I started to crank in the slack there was that familiar jarring strike and we were into a doubleheader.

"Bob, you're sure lucky!" said Rogers. "Those fish must have turned deep and started back toward the boat. You'd have been out in the cold if they had happened

to have gone the other way!"

He was right, and I knew it. The ability to cast accurately for great distances with either spinning or revolving-spool tackle (whichever you prefer) is one mark of the accomplished striped bass angler. With many former surf men taking to boats, and with many boat fishermen taking to casting, skill with the casting rod is important if you're going to take your share of the fish.

Casting ability is no accident. Granted, there are those who just naturally cast better than others. Claude Rogers is better than I am, perhaps because he's taller, stronger, and has longer arms. But you don't have to be a big man to be a Hatteras Heaver. Two of the finest casters I know, Major Kight and Peewee Morse, are both on the slight side.

Good distance casting begins with a good rod. Too many anglers buy rods because the tips vibrate like crazy when whipped in the stale air of a tackle shop.

The salesman watches you fake an imaginary flip to a fish in the shop and begins his spiel. "See the action? It's all in the tip. That'll kill a fish in quick order. The power's in the butt and the action's in the tip. That's a beautiful rod!"

So you buy it, and soon enough you find that it's good only for tossing marshmallows across the duck pond. What the salesman didn't tell you, probably because he didn't know any better, is that when you put a four-ounce lure or three ounces of sinker and a big gob of bait on the end of that rod, the buggy-whip action tip just doesn't have the backbone to toss that much weight any distance.

Flipping a whippy rod in a tackle shop is just like kicking the tires of a new sports car to find out how it handles on the road. If you really like that little sports car, you make the salesman let you take it out to where you can find out if the road-ability is all there, or if it's just a kitten-car trying to snarl like a tiger.

Buy your casting rods the same way. Naturally, few city tackle shop salesmen will let you take an arm-load of samples down to some distant beach, so go to a shore fishing port where boat casters and surf men come for fishing, and seek out a local tackle builder who doesn't know how to build anything but a good long-distance casting rod.

Rent a few rods and use them on the beach or from your boat until you find a model that feels good in your hands and with which you can achieve long, fairly accurate casts. Then buy rods on this model that match your height, weight, and body power. A good tackle man will take pains to sell you only a rod that will perform well after you have learned how to get the most out of it.

Another mistake is to believe that the distance a rod will cast is directly propor-tional to the length of the stick. There are some freakish surf rods available over some store counters that measure up to 14 feet long. Length in a rod is of little value if the stick doesn't have enough back-bone.

A group that has experimented exten-sively with long-distance casting tackle is the Tidewater Anglers Club of Norfolk, Virginia. This fishing fraternity pio-neered the tackle and casting style that first captured the Ocean City (N.J.) Cup, symbolic of national distance casting su-premacy, back in 1958. Virginia teams have won the hardware every year since then to the time of this writing, using the same basic tackle and style.

These casters have found that the ideal rod for casting a four-ounce lead is a shaft measuring just 10½ feet overall. It carries a tiptop measuring 28/64″ inside the tip-top tube, and weighs 35 ounces. Such a rod will handle lures or sinkers ranging from two to seven ounces.

Marion Hutson of Chesapeake, Vir-ginia, used such a rod in establishing a competitive distance record of 490¼ feet, using 36-pound test line, in 1970. Then, shifting to spinning tackle that included 12-pound test mono line behind a short, heavier shock section, Hutson tossed a two-ounce sinker 535 feet in competition.

Hutson is a big, strong fellow and em-ployed a 12-foot rod for spinning that sports a 24/64″ tip-top. Kight, mentioned before, once competitively cast a two-ounce sinker 492 feet with an 11-foot, 7-inch spinning stick with a 26/64″ tip-top.

In distance spinning, one of the biggest drawbacks is the position of the reel with respect to the rod's lowest or first guide. If the line slaps the rod shaft as it comes off the stationary spool, distance is materi-ally reduced by this friction. The same friction loss is experienced at the rod's first guide. If the guide is not almost as large as the diameter of the spinning reel spool, friction can be a real detriment to distance. That is why the first guide is so large, and why guides gradually decrease in size as they progress toward the rod tip.

You can sometimes eliminate the slap-ping of line against the rod shaft by posi-tioning a wooden wedge under the front end of the reel foot. This angles the axis of the spool away from that of the shaft, re-ducing slapping. Experimentation will be needed to determine the exact shape of the wedge.

Let's look at the revolving spool. One of the first laws of casting the beginning caster learns is the old law of inertia. Ob-jects at rest tend to stay at rest and objects in motion tend to stay in motion. If you start your bait or lure moving in the direction of the intended cast before you begin to apply the real power of the cast, distance will be increased. It's like a pitcher throwing the baseball with a proper windup.

The accompanying illustrations demonstrate what I mean. Although the model (myself) uses revolving-spool tackle in this series because I'm primarily a revolving-spool caster, exactly the same style is used with spinning tackle. I cast right-handed as do most people, but left-handed casters can do equally well by reversing my "left" and "right" instructions.

I start with my left shoulder pointed toward the casting target, standing at an almost exact right-angle to the target, facing down the beach instead of toward the water and the target. My weight is on my left foot as I start to point the rod directly away from the target, turning my body to the right while lowering the rod and swinging the lure directly away from me and the target. You might say that this is the start of the windup. As my arms extend fully to the right, my weight shifts to the right foot in a smooth transfer of weight. My eyes never leave the lure, because the start of the power stroke depends on the exact position of the lure in its pendulum-swing away from the target.

I start the cast by driving the butt end of the rod like a javelin toward the target with the shaft parallel to the ground until my right elbow is bent almost closed. My body is twisting during this maneuver and weight is flowing in the line of the cast from the right foot to the left. By now the lure is starting to travel quite fast in the target direction and the real power portion of the cast is about to begin, even though the lure is still well behind my body.

As my right elbow angle comes tight, the arm is extended out, pushing the rod shaft upward and toward the target, introducing bend into the rod. At the same time the left hand pulls strongly down on the rod butt end. The follow-through is carried as the rod tip follows the lure's flight through its trajectory to the target.

There's no way I can tell you exactly when to release the line. This is something you have to learn for yourself with practice. Don't waste effort releasing too fast. The idea is to gain distance horizontally, not vertically up into the sky.

With a spinning outfit, you don't have to worry about thumbing the spinning spool to prevent a backlash. This is a serious problem for some revolving-spool casters. With "conventional" tackle it is good to master the proper casting technique before trying for distance. Then you can add power bit by bit as your arms become stronger and your eyes and nerves steadier.

A revolving-spool reel should have a light plastic spool rather than a heavy metal one. A metal spool is harder to start and stop because of the old law of inertia and weight. Some reels come with aluminum spools which are as good as the best plastic. The lighter the spool, the sooner your thumb will become educated to controlling its spin without fetching a backlash.

It's important that a spinning reel spool not be overloaded or underloaded with line. The spinning reel, of course, level-winds the line back and forth across the spool face by the action of the spool and the bail. A caster using a revolving spool reel must learn to use his thumb to lay the line evenly across the spool face so the line will unspool evenly without throwing loose loops during the next cast.

Revolving-spool reels should have wide, shallow spools rather than narrow, deep spools. With a wide, shallow spool there is less tendency for the spool to over-speed as the line diameter becomes smaller during the cast. Deep, narrow spools have a rapid build-up of spool speed near the end of the cast, an invitation to an over-run and backlash.

Left: Begin with your left shoulder (if you are right-handed) pointed toward the water, and stand at right angles to the line of the cast you plan to make.

Above: Turn your body to the right, lowering the rod while extending it directly away from direction of cast. Your body weight is mainly on your right foot.

Above: As the cast begins, body weight shifts to left foot while body starts to pivot in direction of the cast. Keep your eyes on the lure while you drive the rod lengthwise like a spear from right to left.

Above: Continue to shift weight to left foot as full arm power puts deep bend into the rod and your head rotates toward the true direction of the cast.

Right: In the power stroke, right arm pushes rod away from body while left arm pulls back on end of butt. Body weight is almost fully shifted to the left foot.

Follow-through sees the rod fully extended in direction of the cast. Weight is now entirely on left foot. Thumb on spool controls distance of cast.

In spinning, there's a different relationship between distance and the diameter of the spool. Generally speaking, the larger the spool diameter, the longer the cast with the same lure, rod, and line. As the line on the spinning reel spool becomes depleted during the cast, it has a greater distance to bend in coming off the spool, and thus creates greater friction. Because bigger spools hold more line in proportion to the amount cast out, it stands to reason that they'll cast further.

How many times have you lost an expensive lure because the line popped during the cast? It can happen whether you're using spinning or "conventional" tackle. You can reduce line breakage considerably by adding a "shock line" to the end of the regular line. This is a section of clear monofilament ranging from 60-pound test for the heaviest lures down to around 15-pound test for very light lures and tackle. Some anglers make the shock line only three or four feet long, which seems to defeat its purpose in my opinion. I make mine long enough so I can get five or six turns of line onto the reel spool while the lure is hanging at my normal casting distance of about five feet from the rod tip-top.

There are a couple of good knots for joining lines of unequal diameter. One is the Improved Blood Knot. Another is the Albright Special, sometimes called the Keys Loop Knot. In a pinch the Surgeon's Knot will do. For spinning tackle, coat the knot with successive coats of Pliobond rubber cement until a smooth, non-snagging lump is built up over the knot. This will keep the knot from hanging up in the rod guides.

The overhang of the lure, or the distance that it is allowed to hang down from the rod tip before casting, adds distance to any cast. The overhang will vary with the length of the rod, the weight of the lure, and the local wind condition. Heavier lures usually require more overhang than light lures.

While most of this discussion has been centered around surf tackle, the same basics apply throughout the entire striper casting field. Only when casting with extremely lightweight lures, such as quarter-ounce spinning plugs and light bait-casting lures, will a whippy rod do a better job. For small fish in short-range casting water, my favorite outfit is a seven-foot stick tapering slowly from a 14/64″ tip-top. It carries a bait-casting reel and handles anything from a ¼-ounce largemouth bass popper to a 2½-ounce Hopkins jig.

In summary, here are the main points to remember if you want to improve your distance casting for stripers:

1. Except with very lightweight lures, stiff rods usually give better distance than whippy rods.

2. By the same token, lighter tips give greater accuracy, so don't limit your wardrobe to just one rod.

3. Revolving-spool reels should have lightweight plastic or aluminum spools, not brass.

4. In spinning, large diameter spools give more distance by reducing casting line friction

5. Line should always be spooled level onto a revolving-spool reel. Spinning reels should be filled not more than 1/16″ below the lip of the spool.

6. A shock line will help reduce line breakage.

7. Don't overburden yourself with a rod that's too long or too heavy for your build and power.

8. Distance casting ability is no accident. Style is important and style requires practice and occasional critical coaching from a real expert.

2 4 / Target—A Record Striper

WHEN GUS PIAZZA OPENED THE BOX OF FISH from Maryland at what was then New York's Fulton Fish Market, he let out a gasp of astonishment. Inside was the biggest striped bass he had ever seen. Hung on the market scales, the huge striper weighed 81 pounds—eight pounds over the existing 73-pound all-tackle record set by Charles Church at Quick's Hole, Massachusetts, back in 1913.

To keep it from becoming steaks on some restaurant's menu, Gus bought the fish from his employers and later turned it over to the F. & M. Schaefer Brewing Company, who had it mounted, tangible proof that record-breaking stripers still swim in Atlantic waters.

The quest for a new record striper has been going on for years. Charles Cinto of Mansfield, Massachussets, came close when he tied the Church record in 1967 with another 73-pounder taken at night off Sow and Pigs Reef, Cuttyhunk, fishing with guide Frank Sabatowski. Unfortunately, the fish was denied official recognition by the International Game Fish Association because it was caught on wire line and a gang-hook plug, two items not then sanctioned by IGFA tackle rules.

Cinto is said to have swallowed his chagrin with the observation, "Well, they can't deny that I caught the fish, and that's what really counts."

But recognition of a potential record by the IGFA does mean the supreme accolade to most non-commercial fishermen. How to equip yourself and shape your plans toward the target of an eventual personal, regional, or world striped bass record is the aim of this chapter.

Your first decision should be that of tackle. More times than I care to reveal I have heard anglers complain, "If only I'd been fishing with IGFA tackle, that big fish might have been a record!"

You don't win IGFA recognition with outlaw tackle, so if a record is your aim, get a set of the latest IGFA tackle rules, combined with the current record listings. They cost only $1.25 ($1.75 foreign) and are available from the IGFA at 3000 Las Olas Boulevard, Fort Lauderdale, Florida 33316.

Very briefly, the rules we are interested in here encompass the following major requirements:

1. You may not fish with any form of wire line.

2. You may use outriggers including so-called "downriggers" for deep trolling as long as the fishing line itself is made of soft material such as linen, nylon, Dacron, etc.

3. Your line must test under the top breaking strain for the tackle class in which you enter the fish. The line classes recognized by the IGFA are 6, 12, 20, 30, 50, 80, and 130 pound breaking strain.

4. Your bait or lure must conform to IGFA hook and leader specifications. Rules now permit use of two gang-hooks attached to the body of a plug used for casting, but such a lure may not be used for trolling. Your leader may not measure more than 15 feet long for lines of 50 pound test and under, nor more than 30

Charles Cinto's 73-pounder, caught at Cuttyhunk, is almost as tall as he is.

feet for lines of 80 and 130 pound test. Actually, no one uses leaders 15 feet long except in some special trolling applications.

5. Finally, your fish must be weighed, measured, photographed, and registered in the proper manner and the entry blank forwarded within the stated period of time. A 30-foot sample of line is required for IGFA testing. Over-testing of line, incidentally, is said by the IGFA to be the major cause for rejection of entries.

The various IGFA line classes provide a very wide choice of tackle and fishing techniques and open the possibility of breaking line class records with fish that are not heavy enough to be all-tackle contenders. The best strategy, therefore, is to consider the big striper potential of your favorite fishing area and then to concentrate on a line class of tackle and a fishing method that gives you the best chance for eventual record success.

One general rule supercedes all others. This is the old law that big stripers like big lures and baits. The second important rule to remember is that boat fishermen catch many more big stripers than surf fisherman. This is not meant as a put-down of surf fishing. Rather, it is intended to point out that if a personal, club, regional, or world record is your goal, your chances are better if you fish from a boat.

The exact mechanics of rigging and using trolling and casting lures are described in detail in other chapters of this book. Let us therefore concentrate on where to go, when to be there, and what tackle, lures, baits, and special tricks to use at the spots that have been selected as probably the very top big-striper producing pastures of the East and West Coasts.

Cape Cod Outer Beaches. The outer ocean beaches of Cape Cod, notably in the region from Race Point to North Truro, have produced many very large stripers in recent years. One record was the 64¼-pounder taken off North Truro in 1960 by Rosa Webb to set a new women's 30 pound line class record. Her fish hit a live mackerel. While this part of the Cape Cod beach is a surf fisherman's paradise, most of the really big stripers have been caught by live bait or by plugging from beach-launched cartop or trailer-borne outboard boats.

Ideal boats for this kind of work are 12' to 14' aluminum outboard skiffs that can be launched and retrieved handily by two anglers. Outboard power of 20 horsepower is sufficient.

Rosa Webb's winner was caught in August, but the Cape hosts big stripers on the outer beaches from June through late October. July through early October seems to be the longest good period with peak action fluctuating from season to season depending on the availability of Boston mackerel or other choice live bait. Boats fish first for mackerel by jigging, then bring the live baits inside the outer beach bars, fishing them deep in the slough that exists between outer bar and the beach. Wash tubs or G.I. cans make good jury live bait tanks.

For live bait fishing with mackerel, many anglers prefer a cut-down surf rod that matches 20 to 30 pound class line. Some anglers use spinning reels, but the best live mackerel reel is a 200 to 300 yard capacity level-wind star drag reel with strong, smooth-working drag. A few anglers use deep sea reels of up to 3/0 or 4/0 size, although a slightly smaller reel is lighter and easier to handle. The 6/0 to 8/0 Eagle Claw or similar hook is usually tied directly to the end of the line, although some fishermen use a short piece of heavier shock leader.

Casting rods rigged with swimming, darting, or popping plugs are kept ready in case the fish should start to work bait on the surface. This is most likely to happen in morning or evening twilight, but can take place at almost any hour of the day or night. The majority of anglers seem to prefer a surf spinning outfit with large capacity reel loaded with 20 to 30 pound test mono line.

Surf casters catch many large fish from the shore, but boat anglers seem to get the majority of really big ones somewhat beyond normal casting range from shore.

Billingsgate Shoal and Cape Cod Bay. Shoals inside Cape Cod Bay have produced notable catches of big stripers among the schoolies, and Billingsgate Shoal, off Wellfleet, is one of the most popular shoal areas. Here the most productive fishing method for trophy stripers seems to be the live mackerel technique, although deep trolling and surface casting often work well.

This water may be fished by boats ranging from small outboards up to full-fledged offshore fishermen. As in many other similar offshore shoal areas, the activity of the fish appears to be strongly regulated by the flow of tidal currents. Sometimes the ebb may be better, at other times the flood, but slack water is usually a period of inactivity. The Current Tables should be consulted before making final decisions about the hours to fish.

Tackle requirements are essentially the same as for the Cape outer beaches, except that local charter boats usually use regular star drag boat rods and often run to lines of up to 40 and even 50 pound test. Some boats troll with big feathers and squid or pork rind, large spoons, rigged eels, eelskins, or large trolling plugs.

Be prepared to switch to surface trolling or casting tackle if the fish suddenly start chasing bait on the surface. By the same token, if fast-moving boats drive the surfaced fish down, don't just sit there and cuss. Change over quickly to deep-trolling or live bait tackle and put your lures and baits down where the hungry fish will find them. By recognizing what's going on with the fish you can often use boat traffic to your advantage.

Best time for Cape Cod Bay shoals is middle to late August through October. Weekends often see huge fleets of small boats on the water in good weather, so time your ventures for midweek fishing if you can, and work the dawn and evening twilight periods when the run of the tide is favorable. Be prepared for fog, especially at night.

Cape Cod Canal. Where big stripers are concerned, Cape Cod Canal is a rather specialized location used primarily by surf and shore fishermen in the spring when live herring are available for bait. Herring can be bought from commercial bait dealers, but most fishermen catch their own in the local fresh water streams up which the herring migrate to spawn. The live herring are rigged and fished in the same way that bunkers or mackerel are used.

A three to four foot shock leader of 40 pound material is commonly used, tied directly to the 18 to 30 pound mono fishing line by means of a blood knot. The hook is the usual Eagle Claw, O'Shaughnessy, or treble used for live bait. Herring are kept alive in metal or plastic tanks carried by the anglers in their trucks, campers, or cars.

Plugging and casting eels or metal squids from shore also produce stripers in the canal. The Cape Cod Canal has a variable history of summer striper production and gets good again in the fall when the late-season migration sets in. Some boats fish the canal when weather prevents them from fishing outside in Buzzards Bay or Cape Cod Bay.

Cuttyhunk and the Elizabeth Islands. Cuttyhunk, the westernmost of the chain of islands that separates Buzzards Bay from Vineyard Sound, is probably the most famous single spot in the world for trophy stripers. Here was caught Charles Cinto's record-tying 73-pounder, E. J. Kirker's current all-tackle record 72-pounder, and a host of other monumental stripers. The great 73 pound fish taken by Charles Church in 1913 was caught in Quick's Hole, the tidal passage between Pasque and Nashawena Islands, just east of Cuttyhunk.

This is an area of strong tides, heavy rips, and rough, broken bottom. Traditionally, the biggest Cuttyhunk bass have been taken on rigged eels, eelskins, or eel-covered trolling plugs, although the full gamut of plugs, jigs, and trolling lures has produced big fish.

Trolling tackle runs to fairly stiff boat rods with 3/0 to 4/0 reels filled with 30 to 50 pound test line. Wire is widely used by the local charter skippers for deep trolling, but some of them advertise that they will fish any way their clients desire, including using the salt water fly rod if this is desired. Wire, of course, disqualifies a fish for IGFA recognition.

Casting tackle should be equal to the biggest fish in rough water. Because of the strong tides, live bait is not frequently used. The boat too quickly drifts out of a good fishing area. Fishing with live bait from an anchored boat is almost impossible except at slack tide when the stripers are normally fairly inactive.

Lobster pots are frequent hazards to fishing and local knowledge of the hidden rocks is needed to fish some reef areas safely. Cuttyhunk bass guides are very expert. More can be learned from a good guide in two or three trips than from a score of trips in one's own boat without this kind of invaluable tutoring.

The best Cuttyhunk season is said to be autumn, but oddly enough the really big stripers have been spaced out over the entire season. Charles Cinto's 73-pounder, for example, was a June fish. E. J. Kirker's 72-pound fish, present holder of the IGFA

Could it be a record? The possibility of taking a record striper has caused many anglers to swing to IGFA-sanctioned tackle.

all-tackle record, was taken in October. Charles Church's historic monster ate an eel in August.

Kirker's fish, incidentally, now occupies the niche formerly held by Church's striper through a reorganization of IGFA records. New rules require that only records of fish for which the line had been tested will be recorded in the year-to-year records. Church's record has not been "dumped," but is preserved in a special category of accepted records, the lines of which were not tested for one reason or another.

Martha's Vineyard and Nantucket. Both of these delightful New England islands have the potential to produce new record stripers. The Devil's Bridge off Gay Head, the western tip of the Vineyard, for example, is quite similar to Shagwong Reef at Montauk in structure and tide pattern, and is frequented by Cuttyhunk and mainland bass boats when big stripers are known to be in residence.

Martha's Vineyard mounts a highly successful striper derby each fall, a derby that sees hundreds of mainland anglers arrive to fish competitively for prizes and honors. A great deal of this effort is spent along the island's various beaches and headlands by surf fishermen. The Vineyard is visited more by striper boats from other areas than it is fished by boats based on the island.

Nantucket, likewise, is a surf fisherman's Mecca with miles of attractive beaches and famous striper head-lands, notably Sankaty Head, where rips make up when the tide runs strong. After the spring onset of stripers, big fish action is endemic all summer with action peaking in September and October during the fall migration. Nantucket and the Vineyard have not yet suffered (or benefited) from the heavy striped bass boat fishing traffic that characterizes other prime areas on the mainland.

The Rhode Island shore. Intensity of fishing action alone does not account for the large number of king-sized stripers that have been taken in Rhode Island coastal waters from Narragansett Bay westward to Watch Hill. Despite its pollution, Narragansett Bay is still prime fishing territory with a multitude of passages, islands, river mouths, rocky headlands, and sandy beaches to attract and hold the fish.

Point Judith is a famous location for big bass, both for surf and boat fishermen. From Point Judith westward the beaches are mostly sand, punctuated by occasional inlets such as the famous Charlestown Breachway. This is surf fishing territory, and also prime boat fishing country for anglers with the right boats, tackle, and practical experience.

Surface and deep trolling has always produced many big stripers, but live bait fishing is probably the most effective fishing method for trophy fish. Rhode Islanders have perfected the use of the live eel as a big bass bait and annually take scores of huge fish on this potent bait. The use of herring for bait is restricted mainly to the spring spawning runs of these fish.

Bunkers are used on occasion, but are not as abundant as they are at other more southerly fishing areas.

Typical Rhode Island big bass tackle is a full-sized or cut-down surf rod with reel accommodating line of 30 to 40 pound test. Eel-dunkers sometimes use line of as little as 18 pound test, but most prefer line testing not under 30 pounds. Kelp, rocky bottom, and occasional lobster pots are hazards of the fishing, as are other boats.

Trollers usually prefer the type of boat rod that is now accepted in southern New England as a "bass rod." This is a fairly light, but rather stiff, fiberglass rod mounting a 3/0 or 4/0 star drag reel loaded with 30 to 50 pound test line. Roller guides are the best, as is a roller tip-top. Wire line is very widely used for deep trolling, but the record-minded angler may discover a real secret weapon in the Great Lakes downrigger used as an underwater outrigger with Dacron or monofilament line.

Best trolling lures cover a wide variety of types with lures simulating natural eels or big bait such as bunkers, whiting, mackerel, butterfish, and squid among the most successful. A real sleeper is a large white tuna feather, double-hooked, adorned with a long strip of fresh squid. Pork rind is a good substitute for squid.

Because most New England super-stripers come from Chesapeake Bay stock, they are slower to appear in the spring than smaller fish that have wintered over in local waters. Early or mid-June is the recognized start of big bass action along the Rhode Island shore, although a few big fish are taken in the latter half of May. Action is sporadic and usually confined to night fishing during the summer, but builds to a peak during September, October, and November during the fall migration.

There is no shortage of expert guides at such ports as Sakonnet, Newport, Point Judith, Snug Harbor, and the like. Rhode

*No matter how you slice it, the best chances for setting a new striper record
lie with fishing from boats. These charter boats troll off Montauk Light.*

Island stripers are very much regulated by tidal action and the smart angler does his skullwork with the Current Tables before planning a bass trip. News coverage of Rhode Island fishing is good with excellent reports and forecasts available in many local papers and over local radio stations.

Block Island, R.I. Block Island is one of those unique places that one seldom connects with record stripers until one takes a sharp look at the records themselves. At the time of this writing, three IGFA line class records are held by Block Island fish, more than for any other locality, Cuttyhunk included.

Biggest of this trio was a 61 pound 10 ounce lunker caught on 12 pound line in 1956 by L. A. Garceau. Mary R. Aubry filled the women's 20 pound line class spot in 1959 with a 57½-pounder.

Significantly, Block Island is one place where a dedicated surf caster stands an excellent chance of hooking a record striper. Prime surf territory girds the en-

tire island with the best spots along the eastern and southern shores. High cliffs make for difficult going, one reason why the surf is not overrun by weekenders.

Boat fishermen do well by drifting and casting plugs, eels, or metal jigs into the surf and among the rocks. Poppers, swimmers, darters and divers all seem to work well. Rigged eels are deadly at twilight and after dark. Trolling is most effective when there is color in the water caused by storm swells or rain washing clay down from the cliffs. Otherwise, the extreme clarity of the water in calm weather works against daytime trolling. Best trolling is done at twilight or at night.

Big bass have been taken at Block Island from May to November. Some visiting sportsmen bring outboard skiffs to the island on trailers via the mainland ferries. Others make the run down from Point Judith, R.I., New London, Conn., and Montauk, N.Y. There are only a few good guide boats available on the island itself.

Tackle should be best quality for trolling, casting, or live bait fishing, as has been described elsewhere in these pages. Activity of the stripers is strongly governed by the tides, so a current issue of the Current Tables is a real necessity. Block Island is exposed, but usually offers some sort of lee for fishing in bad weather. As a big striper spot far from the beaten track it has few peers.

Montauk, N.Y. To millions of East Coast anglers, the name of Montauk Point is synonymous with stripers of the biggest variety. This promontory, the eastern tip of the south shore of Long Island, is a way station which the vast majority of Chesapeake fish have to pass on their spring and fall migrations to and from the New England area. Oddly, Montauk has never produced an IGFA record, although hundreds of bass in the over-60 pound class have been recorded over the years.

Big bass action begins in late May or early June along the ocean beach of Montauk peninsula, with the best action here on the flood tide. Big stripers are taken all summer long by surf fishermen and boat anglers, but the most concentrated trophy striper action takes place from mid-October through Thanksgiving in late November. Election Day in early November traditionally ushers in the finest big striper season.

Best trophy bass methods are trolling with bunker spoons or live baiting with bunkers when bunkers are in, deep trolling with various large lures, trolling or casting with rigged natural or artificial eels in rips at morning and evening twilight, and surf casting with large eels or plugs. The Cape Cod method of live mackerel fishing has not been used to any great extent at Montauk, but should work well when mackerel are in. Likewise, the Sandy Hook method of live-lining big bunkers is occasionally used at Montauk with success.

Standard big striper tackle for trolling

Sally Burgess took this 33-pounder from the surf almost in the shadow of famed Hatteras Light on the North Carolina Outer Banks, late in the season.

or casting is used with few exotic variations. Wire line is widely employed for deep trolling, but a few old timers remember the days when the Montauk underwater outrigger was very effective for getting big lures down deep on linen line. Essentially, this was a downrigger operated from a small pipe outrigger, one rig to each side of the boat.

Increasing boat traffic at Montauk in daytime has caused many of the better fishermen to concentrate their efforts on night fishing. The so-called "umbrella rig" with its multiple lures has caught big stripers at Montauk and is popular there, but is not IGFA-approved. The equally popular method of chumming and baiting with clam bellies, a Chesapeake Bay invention, is productive of many small stripers, but relatively few trophy fish.

Long Island Sound. To call Long Island Sound a logical area for record stripers may sound strange to anglers who have never fished there, but in recent years the taking of many big bass well over 50 pounds and occasionally over 60 pounds marks the sound, especially in its western portions, as potential record country.

The method is live bunker fishing and success varies from year to year depending on the availability of both bunkers and big stripers. Many of the big fish are said to be Hudson River stock, which sounds reasonable. Tackle is typical of this specialized live bait fishing, good quality fiberglass rods matched to line of from 20 pound test up. Reels should have a capacity of at least 300 yards of the line selected.

Getting the bunkers often involves finding a free school and snagging individual fish from it with gang hooks. Then the live bunkers, kept in bait wells, are quickly transported to reefs and areas, notably along the north shore of Long Island in the Nassau and western Suffolk County region. There should be comparable fishing off the Westchester and western Connecticut shores, but the intricacies of this specialized fishing seem to be understood best by Long Island fishermen.

The most active season is summer from July through September when bunker schools are present in the sound.

Sandy Hook, N.J. Despite pollution and sometimes intense boat traffic, Sandy Hook, N.J., has produced a large number of trophy size stripers in recent years. The most popular method is live lining with bunkers and a lively bait business has been developed to supply the demands of hundreds of boats needing fresh bunkers for bait.

Preferred tackle is a cut-down surf rod or a boat rod designed to handle line of 20 to 30 pound test, and a level-wind, star drag reel filled to capacity with at least 300 yards of tournament quality monofilament line. The best techniques for live lining bunkers are discussed in the chapter on live bait fishing.

Action begins in May and continues sporadically during the summer until late fall peaks of fishing. Action appears to be dependent on local populations of bunkers to attract and hold schools of big bass. Boats sail from Atlantic Highlands, the Shrewsbury River, and a number of nearby New Jersey towns. Good guides with charter boats are locally available. Sandy Hook is probably one of the most likely areas for fishing for trophy stripers in northern New Jersey or within easy distance of New York City.

North Carolina Outer Banks. In recent years determined fishermen have found out how to hook the elusive big stripers that commercial netters have been harvesting for years along the North Carolina Outer Banks. This is primarily surf casting country, although some boat fishermen are quite successful.

One revolutionary technique is for shore anglers to locate a school of menhaden into which they can cast with metal lures like the Shorty Hopkins equipped with a gang hook in the tail. Live bunkers are snagged from the school, then are permitted to swim free on the hope that they will attract a big striper. Surprisingly, the system works quite well.

Best months appear to be November, December, and January, during which time the weather can be rugged. "Hatteras Heaver" surf rods are needed, sticks 10 to 12 feet long with correspondingly powerful conventional or spinning reels loaded with line of at least 20 and preferably 30 pound test. Bad surf conditions make boat operations at this time of year doubtful at best. The Carolina Outer

Three prime trophy striper trolling lures: bunker spoon, rigged eel, eelskin.

Banks may yield line-class if not all-tackle records to surf fishermen in the near future.

Pacific Coast. A Pacific all-tackle world record would really upset the fishing world, and certainly would help to jar many West Coast fishermen out of their salmon-only syndrome. Because of the special nature of western trophy striper fishing, the subject of pursuing record class stripers in Pacific waters is dealt with in considerable detail in the chapter "Wanted—A Pacific Record Striper!" by Herb Duerksen, elsewhere in this book.

East or west, the man or woman who fishes only for records is a rare individual. Most people fish for fun and are happy to latch onto a record if one comes their way. But most record-holders share one attribute in common. When a record fish strikes they are prepared for what follows.

Being prepared means always using tackle that will stand up to a potential re-cord-breaker. It means being physically and mentally alert to the chances of taking bigger-than-average fish when these chances present themselves. And it means being able to take advantage of good luck when it comes, or to minimize bad fortune when things go wrong.

You may never catch a record striper other than the one that betters your own personal record. But beating your own record is no small feat and brings great satisfaction. This kind of satisfaction is what keeps many devoted striper anglers fishing on through thick and thin.

One of the wonderful things about stripers is that they have little respect for human status. Before them all fishermen are equal. But some anglers are "more equal" because they take the time and effort to be better prepared. This is one phase of the fishing over which you have control. The rest is up to the stripers.

25 / Fly Rod Stripers are the Greatest

A LESSON THAT MANY WRITERS EVENTUALLY learn is never to begin the windup of an article or book with, "Now, to tell the truth . . ." This sometimes seems to create an impression in some readers' minds that much of what the writer has already said is a pack of lies. That's not the impression I want to create in winding up this book.

But I think that any reader who has struggled this far through the book is entitled to know how I finally discovered how to sublimate the intolerable spells of striper fever that still attack me from time to time. Quite truthfully I have found a crutch and that crutch is the fly rod. Let me tell you how it happened.

Some years ago, after a long career of professional sport fishing, I decided to swallow the anchor and devote full time to a new and promising career of writing and editorial work. To make the break permanent, I sold my boat and fishing business at Montauk, N.Y., hoisted an old-fashioned stock anchor on one shoulder, and started inland looking for a new Promised Land.

Finally, in a quiet valley in the hills of southern Vermont a friendly Green Mountain man named Erwin Powers asked me, "Man, where are you going with that funny-looking pickaxe?"

This was the sign I had been waiting for. I banged down the anchor in 30 acres of prime river-bottom land beside a brawley trout brook and started to soak the sea-salt from my socks. For awhile my patient wife, Mildred, and I were so busy we for-

got all about fishing, but a life-long fisherman cannot ignore nearby fish forever, even if they are only little bitty trout.

Until then I had regarded fly fishing the way a truck driver regards sports cars—pretty to look at dashing up the country roads grinding their gears, but not much when it comes to hauling home the bacon. But my Hatteras Heaver surf rod, my deep trolling wire line war clubs, and even my sharpshooting spinning plug rods were hopelessly out of place in the ankle-deep Rock River.

Only a fly rod would do, a local tackle merchant told me. He was kind enough not to smile when I confessed I didn't know a 3X tippet from a weight-forward line. Then I had to learn how to cast all over again. In casting with ordinary salt water tackle, the weight of the lure pulls the line out from the reel. I quickly found out that in fly fishing you have to cast the line, because the fly has no weight at all and just goes along for the ride.

Fortunately, a short but intensive session at the fine Orvis Fly Fishing School at Manchester, Vermont, got me on the right track before the bad casting style I was teaching myself became habit. Mildred, blessed with few fishing vices, took to fly fishing like a bunny to clover. Practice, I soon found out, is the road to casting perfection. I soon learned to ignore the wise-cracking dudes who stopped to watch what I was doing in half-empty parking lots, on freshly-clipped lawns, and over stagnant farm ponds.

Eventually, I fell into the trick of the

Larry Green and George Cox discuss flies that took their California stripers on salt water fly casting tackle.

A typical small, open bass boat is ideally suited to using the salt water fly rod.

double haul and found that I could shoot a big streamer fly 60 or 70 feet toward a selected target. But even though I was beyond the beginner's stage in casting, I still had to break the ice with the fish.

My opportunity came during an October Tournament of the Full Moon at Montauk, the year after the tournament related in the opening chapter of this book. This time Ken Walsh was my fishing partner and my chosen tackle was an eight-foot Orvis Battenkill bamboo fly rod mounting a Number 2 Fin-Nor salt water fly reel loaded with WF8F (weight-forward, weight-8, floating) fly line. The nine-foot tapered leader had a tippet section testing 12 pounds.

Walsh was very patient. He dredged up bass with wire line, jigged them up with diamond jigs, and spooned them up with deep-diving plugs. But I could not catch a fish.

"Why don't you give up?" he finally said. "You're going after them the hardest possible way."

"Yes, I know," I replied.

We sat in the Boston Whaler and ate lunch. I knew I was going about the fishing all wrong. The fish were deep. Ken was taking them with deep-fishing tackle, and I was wasting my time with a floating line. The tide was at high water slack and within a few minutes would start to ebb up inside the Point, back of North Bar.

"Give me one more chance," I said to Ken, "I want to try close inshore up by Blackfish Rock."

"We tried there before and there were no fish," he reminded me.

"Yes," I replied, "but that was on the flood tide. Now the tide's getting ready to ebb and there will be fish."

Ken brought the Whaler uptide of Blackfish Rock and began a long drift close to shore in shallow water. Bait dimpled the water and a few terns were dipping. It looked fishy. I made a long cast and was stripping in the Keel Fly streamer when I saw a swirl in the water behind the fly.

"I raised one!" I whispered to Ken.

"I saw it. It was a rat," he replied.

A rat is a barely legal school striper.

We were drifting by Blackfish Rock and I decided to lay the streamer close to the dark, weed-draped boulder. My arms were tired from all the casting, but I forced myself to relax and go through the motions of a double haul. The line whistled out in a gratifying rolling presentation and the streamer settled to the water like a gull feather.

I began stripping-in. Suddenly the long rod was quivering like a live thing to the pull of a strong little fish. Ken reached for the gaff.

"No, the dip net," I said. "I want to release it."

"Your only fish and you want to release it?"

"Ey-yuh," I replied, the Vermont expression of positive affirmation coming out without premeditation.

Ken netted the 20-incher and disengaged the hook before slipping the fish back into the water. I put away the fly rod after that and helped Ken fill the fish box with prime table stripers for his freezer, back home. But as I worked the big spinning rod I mentally made every cast with the slender Battenkill.

It's been that way ever since. Now my tackle closet is full of powerful salt water fly rods that will handle any line up to weights, and reels that can take tarpon, sailfish, or big bull stripers. When the striper fever rises in my blood I find myself equating the old passion with an urge to take the fish with the new technique.

My anticipation concentrates not so much on the size of the fish and the massiveness of the catch as on the quality of the fishing. I now know that, with patience, I can make the stripers take the flies I decide to offer to them. The mountain comes to Mohammed and there is

Names of flies from photo (reading left to right):
1. Marabou Fly 2. Roostertail Streamer 3. Thompson's Fly 4. Split Wing 5. Caterpillar Wet Fly 6. Bug-Eye Weighted 7. Honey Blonde 8. Mylar Fly 9. Palmered Bass Fly 10. Larry Green Fly 11. Pink Shrimp 12. Shallow Water Fly

Fishing conditions	1	2	3	4	5	6	7	8	9	10	11	12
Shallow tidal flats				•	•		•			•	•	•
Ocean waters	•	•	•	•					•			•
Fast currents				•	•		•	•				
Deep channels				•	•		•					
Sloughs				•	•	•	•		•			•
Tidewater lagoons				•	•		•	•	•	•	•	•
For trolling	•	•	•	•								•
Moody bass				•			•	•	•			•
School stripers	•	•	•	•	•	•	•	•	•	•	•	
River stripers				•			•	•	•			

peace in the fisherman's soul.

Truly, how good is fly fishing for stripers? Not very good if meat on the table or in the freezer is your target, but very good indeed if the challenge of a new and exacting style of fishing is your aim. Learning to cast with the fly rod is surprisingly easy, especially if you have the advantage of a little expert guidance. The tackle is not very expensive and opportunities for good salt water fly casting are widespread.

My favorite striper fly rod is still the Orvis Battenkill impregnated-bamboo eight-footer designed with slow action to handle weight-8 line. Being lazy, I prefer the new rocket-taper or shooting-head lines that let you cast respectable distances in moderate wind with fair accuracy. Several manufacturers now produce fiberglass salt water fly rods especially designed for this fishing.

The important thing in selecting fly tackle is to get a proper match between the rod and the line that the rod is designed to cast. Every rod works best with a particular weight of casting line, and manufacturers now are able to supply combinations of rod, reel, and line that, if properly handled, will give maximum casting performance.

One of the intriguing aspects of fly fishing is that no complete fly fisherman is ever satisfied until he has taken a good fish on a fly or streamer of his own creation. Tying flies is absorbing fun, inexpensive, and creatively satisfying. Stripers hit both streamers and bucktails. The late, great Joe Brooks preferred bucktail flies for stripers and liked the platinum (all-white), honey (all-yellow), and Argentine (blue-and-white) patterns in that order.

Especially good on big stripers are streamers tied to imitate natural baitfish. Here are some samples:

• Honey Blonde Keel Fly is tied with yellow bucktail wing and tail on the pat-

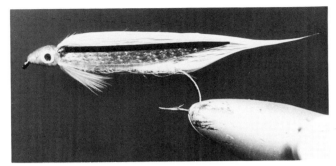

The Maribou Streamer, tied by Bob Zwirz, is a potent striper fly rod lure.

ented Keel Hook with silver tinsel body. Hook size 1/0 to 4/0.

• The Gibbs Striper Fly is tied on a 1/0 hook with no body wrapping; wings of white bucktail; throat of dyed red hackle fibers ¼-inch long; and a cheek of jungle cock breast feathers over blue swan.

• The Jansen Striper Fly is a bucktail tied on a 3/0 hook with body of Mylar tinsel; wing of pale green bucktail over blue bucktail; throat of white bucktail (wing and throat 2½-inches long); head colors of bucktail are made up of matching paint; eye is yellow with black center.

The book *Salt Water Flies,* by Kenneth E. Bay, (Lippincott, Phila., Pa., $8.95) gives precise, detailed illustrated instructions on how to tie 50 popular salt water patterns, including many important striper streamers.

Larry Green, who helped pioneer Pacific striped bass fly rod fishing, has selected 12 favorite striper flies and prepared a special table on the opposite page listing the conditions under which he fishes each model.

Where to go for flyrod stripers? Here are some practical suggestions:

Saco River, Maine, in May and June.

Thames River, Conn., in April and May.

Cape Cod Canal in May and June, September and October.

The Norwalk Islands, Long Island Sound, early summer.

The Hudson River, N.Y., spring and fall.

Charlestown Breachway, R.I., ebb tide, October.

Long Island ocean beaches, June and October.

New Jersey tidal marshes, April to June.

Chesapeake tributary rivers, April to October.

North Carolina tidewater sounds, March to May.

Carolina Outer Banks, November and December.

Santee-Cooper Lake system, spring through fall.

North Florida river systems, spring through fall.

San Francisco Bay, Cal., spring and fall.

Russian River, Cal., March, July, October.

Umpqua River, Oregon, March, July, October.

Lake Havasu, Arizona, May and June, September.

St. Johns River, New Brunswick, June to September.

Annapolis River, Nova Scotia, June to September.

Tusket and Chebogue Rivers, N.S., June to September.

And of course all regular haunts of stripers in ocean or inland waters where the fish school and actively chase natural bait on the surface.

How does the future look for striped bass? Scientists tell us that excellent year-classes in the mid-Atlantic breeding regions in the late 1960s and early 1970s give promise of a high level of population at least to 1976 and possibly to 1980. After that, we shall have to trust to nature and chance that the fish achieve good year classes as time goes on.

Very few stripers caught by sport fishermen are wasted. Still, there is growing sentiment among some sportsmen to release the fish rather than to kill them. I personally see no stigma in taking home fish needed for the table and the freezer, but I also applaud the tagging and releasing of striped bass taken in excess of one's personal table needs. I also applaud the growing trend toward fishing with lighter tackle, increasing the challenge and the quality of the fishing rather than the size of the catch.

Coastal salt water fishermen may soon discover that, in order to continue needed research into and management of important species such as striped bass, they must yield to growing demands for salt water fishing licenses and a mandatory catch limit. Many fish managers question the need for catch limits when populations are high, but an equal number of sportsmen feel that a catch limit is "good for the sport fisherman's soul."

California took striped bass off the market and made them game fish back in the 1930s. On the East Coast, the efforts of some sportsmen to have stripers made game fish throughout their Atlantic range have been successfully thwarted by commercial fishermen who claim that the coastal population of the fish is large enough for all to harvest.

Sportsmen in New York are gathering increasing political clout behind a striped bass game fish effort. It may not be many years before this status is achieved in the Empire State where sportsmen vastly outnumber the few remaining commercial striped bass seine-haulers. But the same does not look promising for the states of the great Delaware and Chesapeake breeding areas, where commercial catches of stripers often are a very important fraction of the states' fin-fish income.

The really important thing is to make sure that our marine scientists keep a constant check on how our Atlantic and Pacific striper populations are making out so that, in case drastic corrective legislation is needed to preserve this valuable species in the future, the groundwork can be laid quickly to obtain whatever protective legislation and management may be needed before it is too late.

Meanwhile, those of us who are sensitive to the virus of striper fever will continue to bless the Good Lord for creating such wonderful fish. Big fish, little fish, in the end what difference does it make? We smell the salt wind spiced with the faint, wild fragrance of bait-fish on which the bass are feeding. We ignore drenching spray, blazing sun, midnight cold. Our reward comes when we feel the first powerful rush of the striper when it responds to the bite of the hook, and later when we lift that gleaming form from the water.

These are the things we remember when the season is over and the fish have departed. These are the hopes that inspire us to renewed faith and action when springtime brings the fish back to us again each year.

Ellis Shires (left) caught these Maine stripers with fly tackle on the Saco River, fishing with guide Jim Trickey.

PHOTO CREDITS

Air bladder. Gas-filled bladder in fish's body used to maintain depth stability.

Algae. Primitive chlorophyl-bearing water plants.

Anadromous. Types of fish that live most of their lives in salt water, but ascend fresh water rivers to breed.

Anal fin. Single fin on lower body surface between anus and tail.

Anterior. Forward part of any object.

Backlash. Tangle of line on reel spool caused by overrun of the spool in casting or dropping-back.

Bait. a) Any natural substance used on a hook to entice fish to bite: b) The act of presenting a lure or prepared bait to a fish: c) Any of a large group of small fishes on which larger fish feed.

Bait-casting. The act of casting a prepared bait or lure by means of a specialized revolving-spool reel and light rod, usually known as a "bait-casting rig." Primarily a fresh water technique, but rapidly growing in popularity in some salt water areas.

Bearing. The direction by compass or azimuth angle of any object as viewed from the observer's position.

Biological clock. Innate reactive behavior of some fish that appears to be regulated by an internal time-sensitive mechanism.

Blitz. Surf caster's term for a fish-catching frenzy.

Bottom fishing. Fishing while anchored or drifting, using sinkers to carry the baited hooks to the bottom.

Bulldogging. Rapid swinging of the head by a hooked fish that sends repeated shocks up the fishing line.

Butt. Lower extremity of a fishing rod below the reel.

Cast. The act of throwing out a bait or lure, using a rod as a lever to give motion to the bait or lure.

Caudal fin. Tail fin.

Caudal peduncle. Narrow portion of tail just ahead of the caudal fin.

CB. Abbreviation for Citizens Band, a civilian radio service operating in the 27 kHz range.

Charter boat. Fishing boat that carries passengers for hire, charging a fixed fee per trip.

Chum. Ground or finely chopped bait that is ladled overboard for the purpose of attracting fish.

Cockpit. The open, sunken after deck of a boat.

Cuttyhunker. Distinctive type of striped bass boat, originally used in the Cuttyhunk Island area.

Demersal. Pertaining to fish that habitually live on or near the bottom of the sea.

Dorsal fin. The prominent fore-and-aft fin on most fish down the centerline of the back.

Double-line. Outer end of fishing line doubled back on itself according to tackle rules to gain strength.

Downrigger. Form of underwater outrigger.

Drail. A specialized trolling sinker with torpedo shape, but with an offset towing neck.

Drag control. The clutch or brake system which allows the line to be drawn out under variable tension.

Drop-back. The act of dropping a trolled bait or lure, or a live bait, back to a game fish so that it may take the bait or lure more readily.

Drop-off. Underwater cliff or bank.

Ecology. Study of the relationship of living species to their habitats.

Estuary. Bay, sound, or large river mouth forming a meeting place between fresh and salt water.

Fathom. Nautical measure equalling six feet.

Fathometer. Registered trademark name for an electronic sounding device produced by the Raytheon Corporation.

Feather lure. Lure dressed with or made up from feathers.

Ferrule. Male or female metal sleeves that form a rod joint.

Fish box. Fixed or portable box in boat to receive catch.

Fish-finder. Electronic sounder.

Fish well. Fish box built under the deck.

Fishing belt. Belt supporting a leather or metal cup or gimbal into which the angler may thrust the butt end of his fishing rod for fishing while standing up.

Fishing chair. Light version of boat chair equipped with rod gimbal and rod holders, for fighting fish sitting down.

Flatfish. Any flounder, fluke, or halibut.

Flat-line. Trolling line fished without outrigger.

Fly rod. Light casting rod that operates on the principle of casting the line rather than the lure.

Flying bridge. Open, elevated control station, usually atop the boat's deckhouse.

Foul-hook. Act of hooking a fish else-where than in the mouth.

Gaff. Strong metal hook attached to a wooden or metal handle, used to hook and lift fish from the water.

Game fish. Any species of fish considered valuable because of its characteristics when caught by hook and line.

Gimbal. Pivoted metal cup equipped with a cross pin, into which a rod butt may be thrust. Usually mounted on a fishing chair or fishing belt.

Guide. a) Person who takes anglers fishing for a fee; b) Metal ring or roller on rod shaft through which the fishing line runs.

Halyard. Light rope or heavy line, usually used to hoist a flag or an outrigger release clip.

Harness. Vest with adjustable straps, worn by angler, to carry weight of rod and fish. Harness straps are clipped into rings on reel frame.

Ichthyologist. Scientist who studies fish.

I/O. Abbreviation for inboard/outboard, or stern drive type of marine proulsion.

Jig. Any small metal lure, heavy for casting or trolling, either plain or dressed with feathers or fibers.

Jigging. a) The act of fishing with jigs; b) Imparting a short, quick, back-and-forth rod action to a trolled lure.; c) Bouncing jig-type lures with an up-and-down motion of the rod, usually in deep water.

kHz. Abbreviation for kilo-Hertz, meaning thousands of cycles per second.

Kite. Special fishing kite used to carry out baits.

Klondike. A great catch of fish.

Knot. Nautical unit of speed, one nautical mile per hour, or about 1.14 statute miles per hour.

Lateral line. Thin horizontal, wavy line visible on the sides of most fish that is a sensitive sound and vibration detector.

Leader. Section of wire or synthetic material placed between the hook and the fishing line.

Littoral. Pertaining to a shore or coastline.

mHz. Abbreviation for mega-Hertz, meaning millions of cycles per second.

Monofilament. Line made of a single continuous synthetic fiber, usually nylon.

Outrigger. Long pole or shaft fastened to side of boat for the purpose of giving lift and separation to trolling lines; usually arranged in matched pairs.

Panfish. Any small, edible fish.

Party boat. Boat carrying passengers for hire for fishing, charging a fee for each person on board.

Pectoral fins. Paired fins closest to the gills on underside of fish's body.

Pelagic. Pertaining to fish that spend most of their time in upper levels of the ocean.

Pelvic fins. Paired fins located on belly behind pectorals.

Pick-up. The act of a fish picking up a bait or lure.

Plankton. Tiny plant or animal life floating freely.

Plug. Wooden or plastic lure shaped somewhat like a fish, designed to be cast or trolled, usually equipped with two or more treble hooks.

Radar. Instrument to achieve radio detecting and ranging.

Range. Imaginary line through two visible objects on shore, extended out over water to the observer's position.

RDF. Abbreviation for radio direction finder.

Reel. Any mechanism for storing fishing line on a fixed or revolving line spool.

Reelseat. Metal sleeve attached to rod shaft, equipped to receive and lock onto the foot of a reel.

Retrieve ratio. Gear ratio of a reel.

Rod. Any tapered, flexible shaft arranged to carry a reel and line, to be used for fishing.

Rod holder. Metal or plastic tube arranged to receive the butt end of a fishing rod while the rod is being used in trolling, or when in the standby condition.

Salinity. Percentage of salt in water.

Seine. Form of vertically hung commercial net.

Shoal. Broad, shallow area.

Shooting head. Special weighted-head-line for fly casting.

Skimmer. The surf or bait clam.

Slick. Thin layer of oil on water surface.

Sound. a) The act of measuring water depth; b) The act of a fish or whale diving deeply.

Sounder. Any depth-measuring device.

Species. Scientific term for a group of identical fishes to which the same scientific name is applied. Species is indicated by the second part of the name.

Spinner. Lure containing a revolving or spinning metal leaf.

Spinning. Fishing method that employs a reel with a fixed spool, the line being laid onto the spool by means of a revolving arm or bail.

Splice. Method of joining two pieces of rope, rope-laid line, or wire rope, by means of inter-weaving strands without using knots.

Spool. The portion of a reel on which line is stored.

Spoon. Metal lure shaped roughly like the bowl of a spoon.

Star drag. Reel drag operated by a star wheel.

Strike. a) The act of a fish attacking a bait or lure; b) The act of an angler pulling back rod and line to hook a fish.

Striking drag. The amount of tension to which a reel's drag is pre-set in anticipation of a strike.

Strip bait. Bait made from a strip of fish, pork rind, or similar material.

Swivel. Low-friction metal connector placed between line and leader.

Tag. Small metal or plastic device fastened to a fish to identify it for scientific purposes.

Terminal tackle. Any part of fishing tackle placed at, or used at, the lower end of a fishing line.

Thermocline. The transition layer of swift temperature change between warm upper water and cold water down deep.

Tide rip. Visible surf-like condition caused by: a) swift current flowing over a bar or shoal; b) two opposing currents meeting.

Tip. Upper flexible portion of a fishing rod.

Tournament. Fishing contest operated according to rules.

Tournament tackle. A grade of tackle considered to be superior by virtue of conforming to special tournament requirements.

Tower. Elevated structure for fishing lookout, usually mounted amidships on sport fishing boats.

Toxic. Poisonous.

Transducer. Device that changes electric pulses into sound pulses, and vice versa.

Trolling. The act of fishing by pulling baits or lures through the water behind a moving boat.

Ventral. Pertaining to the underside of a fish.

Wetland. Coastal intertidal area that is wet at high tide, dry at low tide.

Wire line. Any metal fishing line.